Cartagena
&
Caribbean Coast

Anna Maria Espsäter

Credits

Footprint credits

Editor: Felicity Laughton
Maps: Kevin Feeney

Managing Director: Andy Riddle
Content Director: Patrick Dawson
Publisher: Alan Murphy
Publishing Managers: Felicity Laughton,
Jo Williams, Nicola Gibbs
Marketing and Partnerships Director:
Liz Harper
Marketing Executive: Liz Eyles
Trade Product Manager: Diane McEntee
Accounts Managers: Paul Bew, Tania Ross
Advertising: Renu Sibal, Elizabeth Taylor

Photography credits
Front cover: Dreamstime
Back cover: Dreamstime

Printed in Great Britain by CPI Antony Rowe,
Chippenham, Wiltshire

Every effort has been made to ensure that
the facts in this guidebook are accurate.
However, travellers should still obtain
advice from consulates, airlines, etc about
travel and visa requirements before travelling.
The authors and publishers cannot accept
responsibility for any loss, injury, or otherwise
inconvenience however caused.

Publishing information

Footprint *Focus Cartagena & Caribbean Coast*
1st edition
© Footprint Handbooks Ltd
May 2012

ISBN: 978 1 908206 63 3
CIP DATA: A catalogue record for this book
is available from the British Library

® Footprint Handbooks and the Footprint
mark are a registered trademark of Footprint
Handbooks Ltd

Published by Footprint
6 Riverside Court
Lower Bristol Road
Bath BA2 3DZ, UK
T +44 (0)1225 469141
F +44 (0)1225 469461
www.footprintbooks.com

Distributed in the USA by Globe Pequot Press,
Guilford, Connecticut

Contents

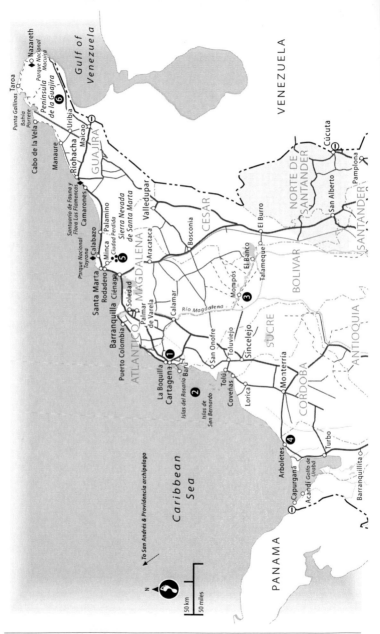

Reaching the lowlands of Colombia's Caribbean coast you enter another world. Steamy, colourful and lively, the entire area pulses to the rhythms of the omnipresent *vallenato*. *Costeños* may be looked down on by their more sombre countrymen, intimating that they lack the same sophistication and work ethic, but they certainly know how to enjoy themselves. There are almost endless fiestas and the Barranquilla carnival is held here, often cited as second only to Rio for colour and size and it's also much less commercial.

Aside from drinking and dancing, there is also fine architecture and an impressive literary legacy, particularly in Cartagena, the emerald in the crown of Colombia. This stunning colonial city is positively bursting with colour and history and offers fine food, a lively nightlife and various sparkling coral islands within easy reach.

South from Cartagena is Mompós, a colonial town where the clocks seem to have stopped somewhere back in the early 20th century. Its main claim to fame is one of the best Easter festivals in the world. Up the Gulf of Urabá, on the way to Panama are the villages of Acandí, Capurganá and Sapzurro, unreachable by road and boasting a wild shoreline of coral reefs and the virgin jungles of the Darién.

Travel east along the coast and you'll reach Santa Marta, Colombia's oldest city and gateway to the spectacular Tayrona National Park. Rising up from the shores is the Sierra Nevada de Santa Marta, the highest coastal mountain range in the world, and one of the few places that can boast tropical beaches and snow-capped mountains within 20 miles of each other. The Sierra Nevada was home to the indigenous Tayrona and a visit to one of their recently discovered cities, Ciudad Perdida, must come high on anyone's list of Latin American adventures.

Beyond Santa Marta is the arid landscape of the Guajira Peninsula, home to the indigenous Wayúu, enormous flocks of flamingos and the ethereal Cabo de la Vela, where turquoise waters lap against a desert shoreline.

Planning your trip

Where to go in Cartagena and the Caribbean Coast

Cartagena is more relaxed than Bogotá, though it is not without the problems of a big modern city. It is colonial Spain's finest legacy in the Americas, impressive in every respect. Spend several days here as there is so much to see. It is also the best base for visits to the Caribbean coast and the islands: check out the beaches and the watersports available. Beaches along the coast and on the offshore islands can be visited, as can the strange mud volcanoes nearby. To the northeast, Barranquilla has its own attractions, including a spectacular carnival, perhaps the finest in Latin America after Rio de Janeiro. Mompós is a superb colonial town that can be visited from either Barranquilla or Cartagena, but you will have to stay overnight. Cartagena is also the gateway to San Andrés, a popular island resort, and to the charming neighbouring island of Providencia.

Best time to visit Cartagena and the Caribbean Coast

The climate varies little in Colombia and, other than the Chocó (northwest Colombia) where it rains almost daily, you will see plenty of sun year-round. There are no seasons to speak of and temperatures are dictated mainly by altitude. The best time for a visit is December to February, on average the driest months. It's worth remembering, though, that this is holiday season for many Colombians and prices rise significantly in the most popular places, and transport, including domestic flights, can be busy. During this period, a number of major annual fiestas are held, for example Barranquilla Carnival in February. Equally, Easter is a local holiday time and almost every town has superb celebrations. In July and August, accommodation prices tend to rise because of school holidays.

Getting to Cartagena and the Caribbean Coast

International flights arrive principally at Bogotá and Cartagena, but there are also direct flights to Barranquilla and San Andrés. Fares are significantly lower in the low season, outside the peaks times of Easter, July, August and December to mid-January.

Transport in Cartagena and the Caribbean Coast

Air

Internal flights are increasingly competitively priced and if you have little time, flying is a worthwhile option. **Avianca**, www.avianca.com, **Aires**, www.aires.aero, **Satena**, www.satena.com, and **Easyfly**, www.easyfly.com.co, are the main carriers, the latter a low-cost airline, with an expanding network of routes. There are also several regional airlines such as **Aerolíneas de Antioquia**, which serve smaller destinations.

A useful search engine for sourcing cheap flights is www.despegar.com. It may be worth using a travel agent to look for flights as they often have discount arrangements with certain airlines, or book online for good last-minute deals, as well as advance purchase fares. **Doble Vía** ① *T211 2754*, and **Vivir Volando** ① *T601 4676*,

Don't miss ...

1 Watching the sun set from the ramparts of Cartagena, page 29.
2 Enjoying the Caribbean on Islas de Rosario and San Bernardo, page 39.
3 Experiencing Semana Santa at Mompós, page 41.
4 Wallowing in the mud volcanoes of Arboletes, page 43.
5 Trekking through the rainforest to Ciudad Perdida, page 65.
6 Learning about Wayúu culture in La Guajira, page 76.

Numbers refer to map on page 4.

www.vivirvolando.com, in Bogotá, and **Destino Colombia** ① *www.destinocolombia.com*, in Medellín and Cartagena, are recommended.

Road
While there are few motorways, the main roads in Colombia are mostly in good condition and journeys are generally comfortable, although landslides frequently close roads after rains.

Bus On the main routes, the bus network is comprehensive and buses are generally comfortable and efficient. Arriving at one of the large bus stations, the choice of carriers can be daunting, but it also has its advantages as there are frequent services and competition between different companies can sometimes allow for a bit of haggling.

There is usually a choice of operators along main routes, with varying degrees of quality and speed. The cheapest, *corrientes*, are essentially local buses, stopping frequently, uncomfortable and slow but offering plenty of local colour. *Pullman* or *servicio de lujo* (luxury) are long-distance buses, usually with air conditioning, toilets and DVDs (almost always violent pirate films dubbed into Spanish). *Colectivos*, also known as *vans* or *busetas*, are usually 12-20 seat vehicles but also seven-seater cars, pick-up trucks or taxis, rather cramped but fast, saving several hours on long journeys. The latter are also known as *por puestos* (pay-by-the-seat) and will not leave until all the places have been filled. It is also possible to order a *'puerta-a-puerta'* (door-to-door) service with some companies. The cost of tickets is relatively high by Latin American standards. Fares shown in the text are middle of the range but should be treated as no more than a guide. These are some of the best known operators: **Berlinas del Fonce**, www.berlinasdelfonce.com, **Bolivariano**, www.bolivariano.com.co, **Copetran**, www.copetran.com.co, **Expreso Brasilia**, www.expreso brasilia.com, **Expreso Palmira**, www.expresopalmira.com.co.

Car With a good road network, self-driving is becoming an increasingly popular way of seeing Colombia. The kind of motoring you do will depend on the car you set out with. While a normal car will reach most places of interest, high ground clearance is useful for badly surfaced or unsurfaced roads and for fording rivers. Four-wheel drive vehicles are recommended for flexibility in mountain and jungle territory. Wherever you travel you should expect from time to time to find roads that are badly maintained, damaged or closed during the wet season; expect delays because of floods and landslides. There is also the possibility of delays due to major roadworks. Do not plan your schedule too tightly. There are *peajes* (toll stations) every 60-100 km or so on major roads: tolls depend on distance and type of vehicle, but start around US$3. Motorcycles and bicycles don't have to pay. For excellent information in Spanish and English, including all the toll costs, see www.viajaporcolombia.com.

Safety: Before taking a long journey, ask locally about the state of the road and check if there are any safety issues. Roads are not always signposted. Avoid night journeys; the roads may not be in good condition, lorry and bus drivers tend to be reckless, and animals often stray onto the roads. Police and military checks can be frequent in troubled areas, keep your documents handy. In town, try to leave your car in an attended *parqueadero* (car park), especially at night. Only park in the street if there is someone on guard, tip US$0.50. Spare no ingenuity in making your car impenetrable. Your model should be like an armoured van: anything less secure can be broken into by the determined and skilled thief. Avoid leaving your car unattended except in a locked garage or guarded parking space. Adult minders or street children will generally protect your car fiercely in exchange for a tip. Be sure to note down key numbers and carry spares of the most important ones.

Documents: National driving licences may be used by foreigners in Colombia. International drivers licences are also accepted. Carry driving documents with you at all times. Insurance for the vehicle against accident, damage or theft is best arranged in the country of origin, but it is getting increasingly difficult to find agencies who offer this service. In Latin American countries it is very expensive to insure against accident and theft.

Fuel: Fuel prices are around US$4.70 per gallon for standard petrol, US$4.10 per gallon for super and US$5.40 per gallon for diesel. Prices are likely to fluctuate in the current economic climate.

Car hire: Car hire, though relatively expensive, especially if you are going to the more remote areas and need 4WD or specialist vehicles, is convenient for touring, and the better hotels all have safe parking. The main international car rental companies are represented at principal airports but may be closed on Saturday afternoons and Sundays. There are also local firms in most of the departmental capitals. In addition to passport and driver's licence, a credit card may be asked for as additional proof of identity (Visa, MasterCard, American Express), and to secure a returnable deposit to cover any liability not covered by the insurance. Check the insurance carefully; it may not cover you beyond a certain figure, nor for 'natural' damage such as flooding. Ask if extra cover is available. You should be given a diagram showing any scratches and other damage on the car before you hired it.

Where to stay in Cartagena and the Caribbean Coast

In Colombia there are a number of quite exceptional hotels that are well worth seeking out. They are usually in colonial towns and not necessarily very expensive. There is a small network of youth hostels, of varying quality and used extensively by Colombian groups, but international members are welcome. Increasingly more budget accommodation and backpackers' hostels are opening up, as well as many chic boutique hotels, often in restored colonial buildings.

There are many names in Colombia for hotels including *posada*, *pensión*, *residencia*, *hostal*, *hostería*, *hospedaje*, *hospedería*, *mesón* and *hotelito*. Ignore them all and simply look at the price range for what to expect. *Motels* are almost always pay-by-the hour 'love hotels' for use by illicit lovers, couples still living with their parents, or prostitutes and their

Price codes

Accommodation

$$$$ over US$150		**$$$**	US$66-150
$$ US$30-65		**$**	under US$30

Price codes refer to the cost of a double room in high season, including taxes.

Restaurants

$$$ over US$20	**$$** US$8-20	**$** under US$8

Price codes refer to the cost of a two-course meal for one person, excluding drinks or service charge.

clients. Most of the time, especially with the more expensive drive-in ones on the outskirts of town, the names will provide an obvious enough clue (eg 'Passion Motel'), but this is not always the case.

The more expensive hotels add on 16% IVA (VAT) to bills. Strictly speaking foreigners should be exempt from this but there seems to be some confusion about the application of this law. Raise the matter with your hotel and you may well get a discount. Some hotels add a small insurance charge.

From 15 December to mid-or late January, and 15 June to 31 August, some hotels in main holiday centres may increase prices by as much as 50%. In some hotels outside the main cities you can only stay (very cheaply) at *en pensión* rates, but no allowance is made for missing a meal.

The Colombian hotel federation, COTELCO ① *www.cotelco.org*, has lists of authorized prices for member hotels, which can be consulted at tourist offices. In theory, all hotels should be registered, but this is not always the case, particularly with regard to cheaper hotels. Most hotels in Colombia charge US$3 to US$10 for extra beds for children, up to a maximum (usually) of four beds per room. Prices are normally displayed at reception, but in quiet periods it is always worth negotiating and ask to see the room before committing.

When booking a hotel from an airport or bus station, try to speak to the hotel yourself; most will understand at least simple English and possibly French, German or Italian. If you use an official tourist agent, you will probably pay a little more as a booking fee. If you accept help from anyone else, you could be putting yourself at risk.

In cheaper hotels, beware of electric shower heaters, which can be dangerous through faulty wiring. Hotels are sometimes checked by the police for drugs. Make sure they do not remove any of your belongings. You do not need to show them any money. Cooperate but be firm about your rights.

Toilets may suffer from inadequate water supplies. In all cases, however, do not flush paper down the toilet bowl but use the receptacle provided. Carry toilet paper with you as cheaper establishments as well as restaurants, bars, etc may not provide it, or make an additional charge for it.

Camping

Local tourist authorities have lists of official campsites, but they are seldom signposted on main roads, so can be hard to find. Permission to camp with tent, campervan or car may be granted by landowners in less populated areas. Many *haciendas* have armed guards protecting their property, which can add to your safety. Do not camp on private land without permission. Those in campervans can camp by the roadside, but it is not particularly safe and it can be difficult to find a secluded spot. If you have a vehicle, it is possible to camp at truck drivers' restaurants or sometimes at police or army posts. Check very carefully before deciding to camp: you may be exposing yourself to significant danger. Some hostels, particularly in rural areas, also offer camping and often provide tents and other equipment at an additional cost, but are still cheaper than dorm beds.

Homestays

In many places, it is possible to stay with a local family; check with the local tourist office to see what is available. This is a good option for those interested in learning Spanish informally in a family environment. However, if you take formal classes, you should have a student visa (see Visas and immigration, page 18).

Youth hostels

La Federación Colombiana de Albergues Juveniles ① *www.fcaj.org.co*, is affiliated to the International Youth Hostel Federation (IYHF) and has 12 hostels around the country, with a main office ① *Cra 15 No 124-17, Torre B, Oficina 201, Bogotá, T612 6422*. Apart from two hostels in Bogotá, there are others, including those in Cartagena and Santa Marta. Hostels are often full at holiday periods, December to January and June to mid-July; it's best to telephone in advance during these times. Otherwise, it's usually possible to arrive without a reservation. Membership can be taken out in Colombia: Hostelling International Cards are recognized and qualify for discounts. See also the Colombian Hostel Association ① *www.colombianhostels.com*, which has hostels in Bogotá, Cartagena, Mompós, Taganga and Valledupar. Hostel Trail Latin America ① *Cra 11, No 4-16, Popayán, T831 7871, www.hosteltrail.com*, is an online network of hostels and tour companies in South America providing information on locally run businesses for backpackers and independent travellers.

Food and drink in Cartagena and the Caribbean Coast

Colombia has yet to reach international renown for its cuisine, but food is becoming more of a draw. Even though you can now find most regional specialities available in all the major cities, there are many local variations to sample in different parts of Colombia.

Some of the standard items on the menu are: *sancocho*, a meat stock (may be fish on the coast) with potato, corn (on the cob), yucca, sweet potato and plantain. *Arroz con pollo* (chicken and rice), one of the standard Latin American dishes, is excellent in Colombia. *Carne asada* (grilled beefsteak), usually an inexpensive cut, is served with *papas fritas* (chips) or rice and you can ask for a vegetable of the day. *Sobrebarriga* (belly of beef) is served with varieties of potato in a tomato and onion sauce. *Huevos pericos,* eggs scrambled with onions and tomatoes, are a popular, cheap and nourishing snack available almost anywhere, especially favoured for breakfast. *Tamales* are meat pies made by folding a maize dough round chopped pork mixed with potato, rice, peas, onions and eggs wrapped in banana leaves (which you don't eat) and steamed. Other ingredients may be added such as olives, garlic, cloves and paprika. Colombians eat *tamales* for breakfast with hot chocolate. *Empanadas* are another popular snack; these are made with chicken or various other meats, or vegetarian filling, inside a maize dough and deep fried in oil. *Patacones* are cakes of mashed and baked *platano* (large green banana). *Arepas* are standard throughout Colombia; these are flat maize griddle cakes often served instead of bread or as an alternative. *Pan de bono* is cheese flavoured bread. *Almojábanas*, a kind of sour milk/cheese bread roll, great for breakfast when freshly made. *Buñuelos* are 4-6 cm balls of wheat flour and eggs mixed and deep-fried, also best when still warm. *Arequipe* is a sugar-based brown syrup used with desserts and in confectionary, universally savoured by Colombians. *Brevas* (figs) with *arequipe* are one of the most popular desserts.

Regional specialities
Fish is naturally a speciality in the coastal regions. In *Arroz con coco*, rice is prepared with coconut. *Cazuela de mariscos*, a soup/stew of shellfish and white fish, maybe including octopus and squid, is especially good. *Sancocho de pescado* is a fish stew with vegetables, usually simpler and cheaper than *cazuela*. *Chipichipi*, a small clam found along the coast in Barranquilla and Santa Marta, is a standard local dish served with rice. *Empanada* (or *arepa*) *de huevo*, is deep fried with eggs in the middle and is a good light meal. *Canasta de coco* is a good local sweet: pastry containing coconut custard flavoured with wine and surmounted by meringue.

Restaurants
In Cartagena you will find a limitless choice of menu and price. Other large towns have a good range of specialist restaurants and all the usual fast-food outlets, Colombian and international. In the smaller towns and villages, not catering for tourists, you'll find a modest selection of places to eat. Watch out for times of opening in the evenings, some city areas may tend to close around 1800 and times may be different at weekends. On Sundays it can be particularly difficult to eat in a restaurant and even hotel restaurants may be closed. Note that more expensive restaurants may add a discretionary 16% IVA tax to the bill.

Most of the bigger cities have specific vegetarian restaurants and you will find them listed in the text. The **Govinda** chain is widely represented. Be warned that they are normally open only for lunch. In towns and villages you will have to ask for special food to be prepared.

The basic Colombian meal of the day is at lunchtime, the *almuerzo* or *menú ejecutivo/del día*, with soup, main course and fruit juice or *gaseosa* (soft drink). If you are economizing, ask for the *plato del día*, *bandeja* or *plato corriente* (just the main dish). This can be found everywhere, many restaurants will display the menu and cost in the window.

The cheapest food can be found in markets (when they are open), from street stalls in most downtown areas and at transport terminals, but bear in mind it might not be safe or agree with you. The general rules apply: keep away from uncooked food and salads, and eat fruit you have peeled yourself. Watch what the locals are eating as a guide to the best choice. Wash it down with something out of a sealed bottle. Having said that, take it easy with dishes that are unfamiliar especially if you have arrived from a different climate or altitude. On the other hand, you may find that fresh fruit drinks, wherever prepared, are irresistible in which case you will have to take your chance! ▶▶ *See Health, page 14.*

Drinks

Colombian coffee is always mild. *Tinto*, the national small cup of black coffee, is taken at all hours. The name is misleading; don't expect to get a glass of red. If you want it strong, ask for *café cargado*; a *tinto doble* is a large cup of black coffee. Coffee with milk is called *café perico*; *café con leche* is a mug of milk with coffee added. If you want a coffee with less milk, order *tinto y leche aparte* and they will bring the milk separately.

Tea is popular but herbal rather than Indian or Chinese: ask for (*bebida*) *aromática*, flavours include *limonaria*, *orquídea* and *manzanilla*. If you want Indian tea, *té Lipton en agua* should do the trick. *Té de menta* (mint tea) is another of many varieties available but you may have to go to an upmarket café or *casa de té*, which can be found in all of the bigger cities. Chocolate is also drunk: *chocolate Santafereño* is often taken during the afternoon with snacks and cheese. *Agua de panela* (hot water with unrefined sugar) is a common beverage, also made with limes, milk or cheese.

Bottled soft drinks are universal and standard, commonly called *gaseosas*. If you want non-carbonated, ask for *sin gas*. Again you will find that many fruits are used for bottled drinks. Water comes in bottles, cartons and small plastic packets, or even plastic bags: all safer than out of the tap, although tap water is generally of a reasonable quality.

Many acceptable brands of beer are produced, until recently almost all produced by the Bavaria group. Each region has a preference for different brands. The most popular are **Aguila**, **Club Colombia**, **Costeño** and **Poker**. **Club Colombia** won the prestigious Monde Selection 'Grand Gold Medal with Palm Leaves' in 2008, marking it out as one of the best beers in the world.

A traditional drink in Colombia is *chicha*. It is corn-based but sugar and/or *panela* are added and it is boiled. It is served as a non-alcoholic beverage, but if allowed to ferment over several days, and especially if kept in the fridge for a while, it becomes very potent.

The local rum is good and cheap; ask for *ron*, not *aguardiente*. One of the best rums is **Ron Viejo de Caldas**, another (dark) is **Ron Medellín**. Try *canelazo* cold or hot rum with water, sugar, lime and cinnamon. As common as rum is *aguardiente* (literally 'fire water'), a white spirit distilled from sugar cane. There are two types, with *anís* (aniseed) or without. Local table wines include **Isabella**; none is very good. Wine is very expensive, as much as US$15 in restaurants for an acceptable bottle of Chilean or Argentine wine, more for European and other wines.

Warning Care should be exercised when buying imported spirits in some bars and small shops. It has been reported that bottles bearing well-known labels have been 'recycled' and contain a cheap and poor imitation of the original contents and can be dangerous. You are probably safe purchasing in supermarkets. Also note that ice may not be made from drinking water.

Fruit and juices

Colombia has an exceptional range and quality of fruit – another aspect of the diversity of altitude and climate. Fruits familiar in northern and Mediterranean climates are here, though with some differences, including: *manzanas* (apples); *bananos* (bananas); *uvas* (grapes); *limones* (limes; lemons, the larger yellow variety, are rarely seen); *mangos* (mangoes); *melones* (melons); *naranjas* (oranges; usually green or yellow in Colombia); *duraznos* (peaches); and *peras* (pears).

Then there are the local fruits: *chirimoyas* (a green fruit, white inside with pips); *curuba* (banana passion fruit); *feijoa* (a green fruit with white flesh, high in vitamin C); *guayaba* (guava); *guanábana* (soursop); *lulo* (a small orange fruit); *maracuyá* (passion fruit); *mora* (literally 'black berry' but dark red more like a loganberry); *papaya*; the delicious *pitahaya* (taken either as an appetizer or dessert); *sandía* (watermelon); *tomate de árbol* (tree tomato, several varieties normally used as a fruit); and many more.

All of these fruits can be served as juices, either with milk (hopefully fresh) or water (hopefully bottled or sterilized). Most hotels and restaurants are careful about this and you can watch the drinks being prepared on street stalls. Another drink you must try is *champús*, a corn base, with fruit, *panela*, cloves and cinnamon added.

Festivals in Cartagena and the Caribbean Coast

García Márquez once said, "five Colombians in a room invariably turns into a party". It could also be said that a couple of hundred Colombians in a village invariably turns into a fiesta. Colombians will use almost anything as a pretext for a celebration. There are more festivals, parties and carnivals in Colombia than days in the year. Every city, town and village has at least three or four annual events in which local products and traditions are celebrated with music, dancing and raucous revelry (these are listed throughout the book). Below are some of the most significant.

January
End Jan Hay Festival Cartagena, www.hayfestival.com/cartagena. A branch of the UK's Hay Festival turns Cartagena into a focus for all things literary during 4 days.

February
2 Feb Fiesta de Nuestra Señora de la Candelaria. Celebrated in towns, including Cartagena, this religious cult festival was inherited from the Canary Islands, where 2 goat herders witnessed the apparition of the Virgin Mary holding a green candle.

February-March
Barranquilla Carnival (movable), www.carnavaldebarranquilla.org. Beginning 4 days before Ash Wed, this is one of the best carnivals in South America. 4 days of partying are compulsory by law and involve parades and plenty of dancing.

March-April
Semana Santa (Holy Week) (movable). Celebrated all over Colombia, but the processions in Mompós are particularly revered.

April
26-30 Apr Festival de la Leyenda Vallenata, www.festivalvallenato.com. One of the most important music festivals in Colombia, 4 days of hard partying in Valledupar culminate in the selection of the best *vallenato* musician.

November
First 2 weeks of Nov Independence of Cartagena and Concurso Nacional de la Belleza. Cartagena celebrates being the first department to win Independence from the Spanish each 11 Nov with parades and traditional dancing in the streets. This has been somewhat supplanted by the National Beauty Pageant in which the winner will go on to represent Colombia at Miss Universe.

Essentials A-Z

Accident and emergency

Police: T112 or 123 (from mobiles); **Ambulance**: T132; **Fire**: T119; **Red Cross ambulance and traffic accidents**: T127; **Centro de Atención Inmediata (CAI)**: T156 (to report theft or other forms of crime and sort out the necessary paperwork). Contact the relevant emergency service and your embassy in Bogotá. Make sure you obtain police/medical reports in order to file insurance claims.

Electricity

110 Volts AC, alternating at 60 cycles per second. A voltage converter may be required if your device does not run on 110 Volts. Most sockets accept both continental European (round) and North American (flat) 2-pin plugs.

Embassies and consulates

For embassies and consulates of Colombia, see http://embassy.goabroad.com.

Health

See your GP or travel clinic at least 6 weeks before departure for general advice on travel risks and vaccinations. Try phoning a specialist travel clinic if your own doctor is unfamiliar with health conditions in Colombia. Make sure you have sufficient medical travel insurance, get a dental check, know your own blood group and if you suffer a long-term condition such as diabetes or epilepsy, obtain a Medic Alert bracelet/necklace (www.medicalert.co.uk). If you wear glasses, take a copy of your prescription.

Vaccinations

It is advisable to vaccinate against polio, tetanus, diphtheria, typhoid, hepatitis A, and also rabies if going to more remote areas.

Health risks

The most common cause of travellers' **diarrhoea** is from eating contaminated food. In Colombia, drinking water is rarely the culprit, although it's best to be cautious (see below). Swimming in sea or river water that has been contaminated by sewage can also be a cause; ask locally if it is safe. Diarrhoea may be also caused by viruses, bacteria (such as E-coli), protozoal (such as giardia), salmonella and cholera. It may be accompanied by vomiting or by severe abdominal pain. Any kind of diarrhoea responds well to the replacement of water and salts. Sachets of rehydration salts can be bought in most chemists and can be dissolved in boiled water. If the symptoms persist, consult a doctor. Tap water in the major cities is in theory safe to drink but it may be advisable to err on the side of caution and drink only bottled or boiled water. Avoid having ice in drinks unless you trust that it is from a reliable source.

Mosquitoes are more of a nuisance than a serious hazard but some, of course, are carriers of serious diseases such as **malaria**, so it is sensible to avoid being bitten as much as possible. Sleep off the ground and use a mosquito net and some kind of insecticide. Mosquito coils release insecticide as they burn and are available in many shops, as are tablets of insecticide, which are placed on a heated mat plugged into a wall socket.

Money → *US$1 = 1763 pesos; UK£1 =2855 pesos; €1=2340 pesos (May 2012)* .
Colombia's currency is the *peso*. The following denominations of banknotes circulate: 50,000, 20,000, 10,000, 5000, 2000 and 1000, as well as coins worth 500, 200, 100 and 50. Large bills may be hard to use in small towns so carry plenty of notes in small dominations (10,000 and below).

Watch out for forged notes. The 50,000-peso note should smudge colour if it is real, if not, refuse to accept it.

Always carry some US$ cash; they will work when and where all else fails.

ATMs and credit cards
As it is unwise to carry large quantities of cash in Colombia, credit cards are widely used, especially MasterCard and Visa; Diners Club is also accepted. American Express (Amex) is only accepted in expensive places in Bogotá. There are ATMs for Visa and MasterCard everywhere but you may have to try several machines before you find one that works. Most **Carulla** and **Exito** supermarkets have ATMs.

The ATM system is different to banks in Europe; the machine does not retain your card during the withdrawal. Insert your card for scanning and withdraw immediately, then proceed as normal. If your card is not immediately given back, do not proceed with the transaction and do not type in your pin number. Money has been stolen from accounts when cards have been retained.

ATMs dispense a frustratingly small amount of cash at a time. The maximum withdrawal is often 300,000 pesos (about US$150), which can accrue heavy bank charges over a period of time. For larger amounts try **Davivienda** (500,000 pesos per visit) and **Bancolombia** (400,000 per visit).

Credit card loss or theft: Visa call collect to T0800-891 725; MasterCard T0800-964767.

Note Only use ATMs in supermarkets, malls or where a security guard is present. Don't ask a taxi driver to wait while you use an ATM.

Exchange
Cash (preferably US$ or euro) and TCs can, in theory, be exchanged in any bank, except the **Banco de la República**. In smaller places it's best to go early; take your passport.

In most sizeable towns there are *casas de cambio*, which are quicker to use than banks but sometimes charge higher commission. US$ and euro are readily accepted; other currencies can be harder to change.

Hotels may give very poor rates of exchange, especially if you are paying in dollars. It is dangerous to change money on the streets and you may well be given counterfeit pesos. Also in circulation are counterfeit US$ bills. You must present your passport when changing money (a photocopy is not normally accepted).

When leaving Colombia, try to sell your pesos before or at the border, as it may be difficult to change them in other countries.

Traveller's cheques
When changing TCs, you will need to show your passport and you may be asked for a photocopy (take a supply of photocopies with you). The procedure is always slow, sometimes involving finger printing and photographs. The best currency to take is US$; preferably in small denominations. Banks may be unwilling to change TCs in remote areas, so always have some local currency (and US$ for emergencies). TCs are not normally accepted in hotels, restaurants or shops.

Cost of living
Prices are generally lower than Europe and North America for services and locally produced items, but more expensive for imported and luxury goods. Modest, basic accommodation costs about US$10-12 per person per night in Bogotá, Cartagena or Santa Marta, but a few dollars less elsewhere. A *menú del día* (set lunch) costs about US$2-3 and breakfast US$1.75-2. A la carte meals are usually good value and fierce competition keeps prices relatively low. Internet cafés charge US$1-4 per hr.

Opening hours
Business hours are generally Mon-Fri 0800-1200, 1400-1700, Sat 0900-1200.

A longer siesta may be taken in small towns and tropical areas. **Banks** in larger cities do not close for lunch. Most businesses such as banks and airline offices close for official holidays while **supermarkets** and street markets may stay open.

Police and the law

You are required to carry your passport at all times. In the event of a vehicle accident in which anyone is injured, all drivers involved are usually detained until blame has been established, which may take several weeks. Never offer to bribe a police officer. If an official suggests that a bribe must be paid before you can proceed on your way, be patient and they may relent. In general, however, there are few hassles and most police are helpful to travellers.

Public holidays

1 Jan New Year's Day
6 Jan Epiphany
19 Mar St Joseph
Easter Maundy Thursday; Good Friday
1 May Labour Day
May Ascension Day (6 weeks and a day after Easter Sunday)
May/Jun Corpus Christi (9 weeks and a day after Easter Sunday)
29 Jun Saint Peter and Saint Paul
30 Jun Sacred Heart
20 Jul Independence Day
7 Aug Battle of Boyacá
15 Aug Assumption
12 Oct Columbus' arrival in America
1 Nov All Saints' day
11 Nov Independence of Cartagena
8 Dec Immaculate Conception
25 Dec Christmas Day

Safety

The vast majority of Colombians are polite, honest and will go out of their way to help visitors and make them feel welcome. In general, anti-gringo sentiments are rare.

Drugs and scams

Visitors should keep in mind that Colombia is part of a major cocaine-smuggling route and avoid any involvement.

There have been reports of travellers being victims of *burundanga*, a drug obtained from a white flower, native to Colombia. At present, the use of this drug appears to be confined to major cities. It is very nasty, almost impossible to see or smell. It leaves the victim helpless and at the will of the culprit. Usually, the victim is taken to ATMs to draw out money. Be wary of accepting cigarettes, food and drink from strangers at sports events or on buses. In bars watch your drinks very carefully.

Other Colombian scams may involve fake police and taxicabs and there are variations in most major cities.

Guerrillas

The government has had considerable success in its fight against left-wing guerrillas such as the **FARC**, but the internal armed conflict in Colombia is almost impossible to predict and the security situation changes from day to day. For this reason, it is essential to consult with locals for up-to-date information. Taxi and bus drivers, local journalists, soldiers at checkpoints, hotel owners and Colombians who actually travel around their country are usually good sources of information.

Hotel security

The cheapest hotels are usually found near markets and bus stations but these are also the least safe areas of most Colombian towns. Look for something a little better if you can afford it, and if you must stay in a suspect area, try to return to your hotel before dark. If you trust your hotel, then you can leave any valuables you don't need in their safe-deposit box, but always keep an inventory of what you have deposited. An alternative to leaving valuables with the hotel administration is to lock everything in your pack and secure that in your room. Even in an apparently safe hotel, never leave valuable objects strewn about your room.

Theft

Pickpockets, bag snatchers and bag slashers are always a hazard for tourists, especially in crowded areas such as markets or the downtown cores of major cities. You should likewise avoid deserted areas, such as parks or plazas after hours. Be especially careful arriving at or leaving from bus stations. As a rule these are often the most dangerous areas of most towns and are obvious places to catch people carrying a lot of important belongings.

Leave unnecessary documents and valuables at home. Those you bring should be carried in a money-belt or pouch, including your passport, airline tickets, credit and debit cards. Hide your main cash supply in several different places. Never carry valuables in an ordinary pocket, purse or day-pack. Keep cameras in bags or day-packs and generally out of sight. Do not wear expensive wrist watches or jewellery. If you are wearing a shoulder-bag or day-pack in a crowd, carry it in front of you.

Women travellers

Unaccompanied foreign women may be objects of some curiosity. Don't be unduly scared – or flattered. Avoid arriving anywhere after dark. Remember that for a single woman a taxi at night can be as dangerous as wandering around alone. If you accept a social invitation, make sure that someone knows the address and the time you left. Ask if you can bring a friend (even if you do not). As elsewhere, watch your alcohol intake at parties with locals, especially if you are on your own. A good general rule is to always look confident and pretend you know where you are going, even if you do not. Don't tell strangers where you are staying.

Time

GMT -5 all year round.

Tourist information

Contact details for tourist offices and other information resources are given in the relevant sections throughout the text. The Colombian government is making a big push to promote tourism and most *alcaldías* (municipalities) have some sort of tourist office, whose staff are invariably very helpful but resources available and standards of service vary enormously in smaller towns. Useful website: www.colombia.travel has plenty of up-to-date and useful information.

Websites

www.clubhaciendasdelcafe.com
Extensive list of coffee *fincas* in the Zona Cafetera.
www.colombianhostels.com.co Network of Colombian backpackers' hostels.
www.conexcol.com Colombian search engine covering many topics. (Spanish only)
www.despegar.com Cheap flights website for travel within Latin America.
www.gobiernoenlinea.gov.co Government website with information on new laws and citizen rights, in Spanish and English.
www.hosteltrail.com/colombia Reviews of hostels, tour agencies and destinations.
www.ideam.gov.co Weather and climate information.
www.igac.gov.co Instituto Geográfico Agustín Codazzi Official maps of Colombia.
www.invias.gov.co Instituto Nacional de Vías (National Road Institute). Current details on the state of the roads with maps, etc.
www.lab.org.uk Latin American Bureau site, based in the UK. Publishes books and holds talks on Latin American issues.
www.poorbuthappy.com/colombia Closed down in Apr 2010, but the archives are still available online. Increasingly out of date.

**www.posadasturisticasdecolombia.
com.co** Information on places to stay in
Colombia, including the Chocó.
www.presidencia.gov.co
The government website.
www.quehubo.com Listings.

Visas and immigration

When entering the country, you will be given
a copy of your DIAN (customs) luggage
declaration. Keep it safe; you may be asked for
it when you leave. If you receive an entry card
when flying in and lose it while in Colombia,
apply to any **DAS** office (see Visa extensions,
below) who should issue one and re-stamp
your passport for free. Normally, passports are
scanned by a computer and no landing card
is issued, but passports still must be stamped
on entry. Note that to leave Colombia you
must get an exit stamp from the **DAS**. They
often do not have offices at the small border
towns, so try to get your stamp in a main city.

It is highly recommended that you
photocopy your passport details, including
entry stamps which, for added insurance,
you can have witnessed by a notary. Always
carry a photocopy of your passport with
you, as you may be asked for identification.
This is a valid substitute for most purposes
though not, for example, for cashing TCs
or drawing cash across a bank counter.
Generally acceptable for identification
(eg to enter government buildings) is a
driving licence, provided it is plastic, of credit
card size and has a photograph. For more
information, check with your consulate.

Tourist visas

Tourists are normally given 30 days
permission to stay on entry. If you intend to
stay more than 30 days, make sure you ask
for longer and you can be granted up to
90 days, but 60 days is more common.

Nationals of Bulgaria, Russia and the
Middle East (except Israel), Asian countries
(except Japan, South Korea, Philippines,
Indonesia and Singapore), Haiti, Nicaragua,
and all African countries need a visa to visit
Colombia. If in doubt, check regulations
before leaving your home country. Visas
are issued only by Colombian consulates.
When a visa is required you must present
a valid passport, 3 photographs on white
background, the application form (in
duplicate), US$13-40 or equivalent (price
varies according to nationality), onward
tickets, and a photocopy of all the
documents (allow 2 weeks maximum).

Visa extensions

If not granted at the border, an extension
(*salvoconducto*) can be applied for at the
DAS (security police) office in any major city.
The *salvoconducto* is only issued once for a
period of 30 days, costs around US$36 and is
usually processed within 24 hrs. It is best to
apply 2-3 days before your visa expires. Bring
2 recent photos and copies of your passport.
If you overstay on any type of visa, you will
be charged a fine, minimum US$55 up to
US$800. The **DAS** office in Bogotá is Cra 28
No 17A-00, T408 8000, www.das.gov.co.
Arrive early in the morning, expect long
queues and a painfully slow bureaucratic
process. DAS does not accept cash payments;
these are made at the appropriate bank with
special payments slips.

Alternatively, if you have good reason to
stay longer (eg for medical treatment), apply
at the embassy in your home country before
leaving. If you wish to stay between 7-10
days longer on a tourist visa, go to a DAS
office with your onward ticket and they will
usually grant you a free extension on the
spot. An onward ticket may be asked for at
land borders or Bogotá international airport.
You may be asked to prove that you have
sufficient funds for your stay.

Weights and measures

Colombia uses the metric system, but US
gallons for petrol.

Contents

Footprint features

Cartagena & Caribbean Coast

At a glance

⊖ **Getting around** Walking in city centre. Buses and taxis between cities.

◉ **Time required** 2-3 weeks to explore Cartagena, Santa Marta and other regions.

☼ **Weather** Hot all year round; more rain Aug-Nov.

⊗ **When not to go** Very crowded during Christmas and Easter periods but most festivals occur during this time.

Cartagena

Cartagena is one of the hottest, most vibrant and beautiful cities in South America, combining as it does superb weather, a sparkling stretch of the Caribbean and an abundance of tropical fruits. Nuggets of history can be found around every corner and in every palm-shaded courtyard of this most romantic of places. With exquisitely preserved colonial mansions, excellent museums and fine dining, it's a place not to be missed.

Arriving in Cartagena

Getting there
Rafael Núñez airport is 1.5 km from the city in the Crespo district and it can be reached by local buses from Monumento India Catalina, in the northeast corner of the inner wall and along Avenida Blas de Lezo. There are two *casas de cambio*, one in the international terminal and one in the domestic (T656 4943, Monday-Friday 0830-2030, Saturday 0830-1700 and Sunday 0830-2100). It cashes Amex TCs but not Bank of America and better rates are available in town. For tourist information, ask at the travel agent's offices on the upper level. There is also a good self-service restaurant. A bus from the airport to Plaza San Francisco costs between US$0.70 and US$0.90, depending on whether the bus is air-conditioned. A taxi to the centre is US$7.50 (official price). Buses and taxis for the return trip can be found on Avenida Blas de Lezo close to Puerta del Reloj. Buses can be very crowded and if you have a lot of luggage, a taxi is recommended.

The **bus terminal** is 30 minutes away from town on the road to Barranquilla, a taxi costs US$7.50, or you can take the city buses to the 'Terminal de Transportes', from between US$0.70 and US$0.90. Agree your taxi fare before you get in.

Undoubtedly the best way to arrive is by sea and a description of the approach is given below, under Background. Regular lines are at present non-existent, but what is possible is detailed under Transport, on page 37. Cartagena is, however, popular for cruise ships and those who have their own sea transport: around 345,000 passengers pass through the docks each year. Equally, many tourists take trips to the offshore islands.

Getting around
Local buses are crowded, slow and ramshackle but also colourful, cheap and a good way to see the locals. As usual in Latin America, do watch your belongings. **Taxis** are also quite cheap and more convenient. There are no metres, journeys are calculated by zones, each zone costing about US$1.40, though the minimum fare is US$3. Thus Bocagrande to Centro, two zones, is US$3. It is quite common to ask other people waiting if they would like to share, but, in any case, always agree the fare with the driver before getting in. By arrangement, taxis will wait for you if visiting more remote places. Fares go up at night.

Best time to visit
The climate varies little during the year. Temperatures rise marginally when there is more frequent rain (August-November), and there can be flooding. Freak weather is very unusual, but almost all of Colombia suffered from unusually long and heavy rains during 2010, with some of the coast severely affected, although not Cartagena itself. Fiestas are

taken seriously in Cartagena, and if you want a quiet time you might want to avoid certain times of the year. If you want to join in, be sure to plan in advance or be prepared to struggle for accommodation and expect higher prices. ➻ *For further information, see Festivals, page 35.*

Tourist information

Turismo Cartagena de Indias ① *www.turismocartagenadeindias.com,* has 5 offices; the main one is in the **Plaza de la Aduana** ① *T660 1583, Mon-Sat 0900-1300 and 1400-1800, Sun 0900-1700*, with very helpful and knowledgeable staff, and there are kiosks in Plaza de los Coches, Plaza de San Pedro Claver, at the airport and along the Muelle Turístico where the day-trip and excursion boats leave from. The Colombian Tourist Board, **Proexport** ① *C 28, No 13A-15, p35, T560 0100, www.colombia.travel*, is another useful source of information.

Security

Carry your passport, or a photocopy, at all times. Failure to present it on police request can result in imprisonment and fines. Generally, the central areas are safe and friendly (although Getsemaní is less secure), but should you require the police, there is a station in Barrio Manga. Beware of drug pushers on the beaches, pickpockets in crowded areas and bag/camera snatchers on quiet Sunday mornings. At the bus station, do not be pressurized into a hotel recommendation different from your own choice.

Background

The full name of Cartagena is Cartagena de Indias, a name that is quite frequently used and a reminder that the early Spanish navigators believed they had reached the Far East. It was founded by Pedro de Heredia on 13 January 1533. The core of the city was built by the Spaniards on an island separated from the mainland by marshes and lagoons close to a prominent hill, a perfect place for a harbour and, more important at the time, easy to defend against attack. Furthermore, it was close to the mouth of the Río Magdalena, the route to the interior of the continent. In 1650, the Spaniards built a connection to the river, 145 km long, known as the **Canal del Dique**, to allow free access for ships from the upriver ports. This waterway has been used on and off ever since, was updated in the early 19th century and it is still used, mainly by barges, today.

The great Bay of Cartagena, 15 km long and 5 km wide is protected by several low, sandy islands. There were then two approaches to it, Bocagrande, at the northern end of Tierrabomba island – this was the direct entry from the Caribbean – and Bocachica, a narrow channel to the south of the island. Bocagrande was blocked by an underwater wall after Admiral Vernon's attack in 1741, thus leaving only one, easily protected, entrance to the approach to the harbour. The old walled city lies at the north end of the Bahía de Cartagena.

Cartagena declared its Independence from Spain in 1811. A year later Bolívar used the city as a jumping-off point for his Magdalena campaign. After heroic resistance, Cartagena was retaken by the royalists under General Pablo Morillo in 1815. It was finally freed by the patriots in 1821.

Cartagena today

Although Cartagena is Colombia's fifth largest city, the short-term visitor will not be aware of the size of the place. Beyond and behind the old walled city, Bocagrande and Manga, is a large sprawling conurbation that stretches 10 km to the southeast. People have been moving in to add to the pressure on the poorer neighbourhoods as everywhere else in this part of the world, but Cartagena is a long way from the more heavily populated parts of highland Colombia, to the city's advantage.

Places in Cartagena → *Phone code 5. Population: 1,200,000.*

The city's fortifications

Cartagena was one of the storage points for merchandise from Spain and for treasure collected from the Americas to be sent back. A series of forts protecting the approaches from the sea, and the formidable walls built around the city, made it almost impregnable.

Entering the **Bahía de Cartagena** by sea through Bocachica, the island of Tierrabomba is to the left. At the southern tip of Tierrabomba is the fortress of **San Fernando**. Opposite it, right on the end of Barú island, is the **Fuerte San José**. The two forts were once linked by heavy chains to prevent surprise attacks by pirates. Barú island is separated from the mainland only by the Canal del Dique. In recent years, the city has been expanding down the coast opposite Tierrabomba and settlements can be seen as you approach the entrance to the inner harbour of Cartagena, protected by another two forts, **San José de Manzanillo** on the mainland and the **Fuerte Castillo Grande** on the tip of **Bocagrande**, now the main beach resort of the city.

In the centre of the harbour is the statue of the Virgin with the port installations to the right on Manga Island. There is a very good view of the harbour, cruise boats and port activity from the end of Calle 6/Carrera 14, Bocagrande, though access to Castillo Grande itself is restricted. Manga Island is now an important suburb of the city. At its northern end a bridge, **Puente Román**, connects it with the old city. This approach to the city was defended by three forts: **San Sebastián del Pastelillo** built between 1558 and 1567 (the Club de Pesca has it now) at the northwestern tip of Manga Island; the fortress of **San Lorenzo** near the city itself; and the very powerful **Castillo San Felipe de Barajas** ① *open daily 0800-1800, US$7.50*, inland on San Lázaro hill, 41 m above sea-level, to the east of the city.

The first fortifications on the site were built in 1536 though the main constructions began in 1639 and it was finished by 1657. It is the largest Spanish fort built in the Americas. Under the huge structure is a network of tunnels cut into the rock, lined with living rooms and offices. Some are open and illuminated, a flashlight will be handy in the others; visitors pass through these and on to the top of the fortress. Good footwear is advisable in the damp sloping tunnels. Baron de Pointis, the French pirate, stormed and took it, but Admiral Vernon failed to reach it. In the **Almacén de Pólvora** (Gunpowder store), there is an interesting 1996 reproduction of Vernon's map of the abortive attempt to take the city in 1741. On the statue of Don Blas de Lezo below the fortress, don't miss the plaque displaying the medal prematurely struck celebrating Vernon's 'victory'.

Yet another fort, **La Tenaza**, protected the northern point of the walled city from a direct attack from the open sea. The huge encircling walls were started early in the 17th century and finished by 1735. They were on average 12 m high and 17 m thick, with six gates. Besides barracks, they contained a water reservoir.

Around the old city

The old walled city was in two sections, outer and inner. Much of the wall between the two disappeared some years ago. Nearly all the houses are of one or two storeys. In the outer city, the artisan classes lived in the one-storey houses of **Getsemaní** where many colonial buildings survive. Today, there is a concentration of hotels and restaurants here. Immediately adjoining is the modern downtown sector, known as **La Matuna**, where vendors crowd the pavements and alleys between the modern commercial buildings. Several middle range hotels are in this district, between Avenidas Venezuela and Lemaitre.

In the **inner** city, the houses in **El Centro** were originally occupied by the high officials and nobility. **San Diego** (the northern end of the inner city) was where the middle classes lived: the clerks, merchants, priests and military. Today, the streets of the inner city are relatively uncrowded; upmarket hotels and restaurants are sprinkled throughout the area.

Just under a kilometre from the old city, along a seafront boulevard, **Bocagrande** is a spit of land crowded with hotel and apartment towers. Thousands of visitors flock to the beach with its accompanying resort atmosphere, fast-food outlets, shops – and dirty seawater. See Beaches, page 30.

The old city streets are narrow. Each block has a different name, a source of confusion, but don't worry: the thing to do is to wander aimlessly, savouring the street scenes, and allow the great sights to catch you by surprise. However, if you do want to know what you are looking at, the maps are marked with numerals for the places of outstanding interest. Most of the 'great houses' can be visited. Churches are generally open to the public at 1800, some for most of the day. Weekends and holidays are the best time for photography when traffic is minimal. What follows is a walking route for the sights of the old city which you can pick up and leave wherever you wish. Note that the numbers below refer to the circled numbers on the Historical Centre map.

Outer city

The **Puente Román** (1) is the bridge which leads from Manga Island, with its shipping terminals, into Getsemaní, characterized by its *casas bajas* (low houses). The chapel of **San Roque** (2), early 17th century, is near the end of Calle Media Luna, and the hospital of Espíritu Santo. Just across the Playa Pedregal (3) is the Laguna de San Lázaro and the **Puente Heredia**, on the other side of which is the Castillo San Felipe de Barajas, see above. In an interesting plaza, is the church of **La Santísima Trinidad** (4), built 1643 but not consecrated until 1839, now gently crumbling. West of the church, at No 10 Calle Guerrero, lived Pedro Romero, who set the revolution of 1811 going by coming out into the street shouting 'Long Live Liberty'. His statue can be seen outside La Santísima Trinidad. Along Calle Larga (5), Calle 25, is the monastery of **San Francisco**. The church was built in 1590 after the pirate Martin Côte had destroyed an earlier church built in 1559. The first Inquisitors lodged at the monastery. From its courtyard a crowd surged into the streets claiming Independence from Spain on 11 November 1811. The main part of the monastery has now been turned into business premises – take a look at the cloister garden as you pass by. Handicrafts are sold in the grounds of the monastery, good value, fixed prices, and, at the back, is the Centro Comercial Getsemaní, a busy shopping centre. On the corner of Calle Larga, formerly part of the Franciscan complex, is the **Iglesia de la Tercera Orden**, a busy church with a fine wooden roof of unusual design and some brightly painted niche figures. The church and monastery front on to the Avenida del

Cartagena historical centre

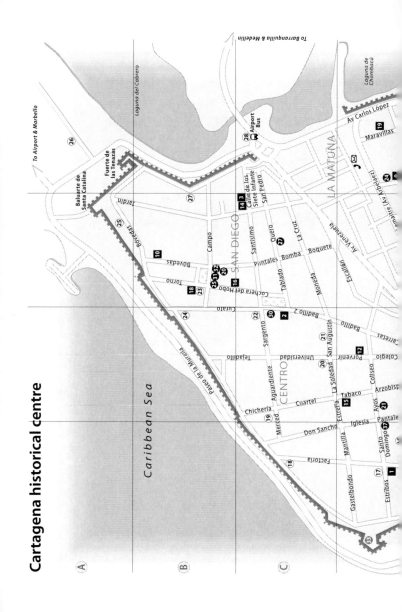

To Airport & Marbello

To Barranquilla & Medellín

Laguna del Cabrero

Laguna de Chambacú

Baluarte de Santa Catalina

Fuerte de las Tenazas

Airport Bus

Av Carlos López

Maravillas

LA MATUNA

Av Venezuela

Pedro de Heredia (Av Arbeláez)

Jardín

Bóvedas

Campo

SAN DIEGO

Calle de los Siete Infante
San Pedro

Santísimo

Quero

La Cruz

Piñtales Bomba Boquete

Moneda

Escallón

Torno

Cochera del Hobo

Tablado

Badillo 2

Badillo

Carreras

Paseo de la Muralla

Curato

Sargento

Tejadillo

Universidad

San Augustín

Porvenir

Colegio

Coliseo

Caribbean Sea

Aguardiente

Merced

La Soledad

CENTRO

Cuartel

Chichería

Tabaco

Estrella

Arzobisp

Ayos

Pantale

Don Sancho

Iglesia

Santo Domingo

Mantilla

Factoría

Gastelbondo

Estribós

3

14
27

10

23 31 32
20
16
18
23

22
30
2

21
12

20

15
28

19

26

25

24

17
18

1

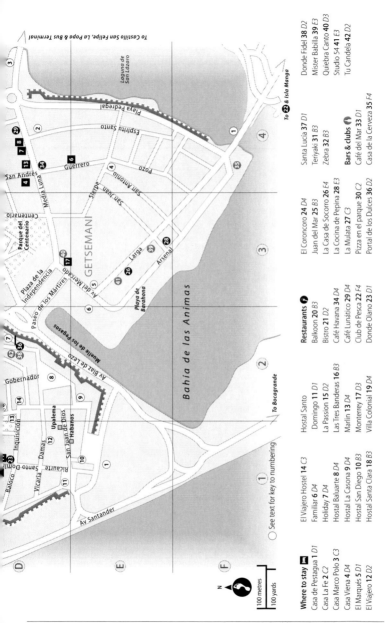

To Castillo San Felipe, La Popa & Bus Terminal

Laguna de San Lázaro

To 22 & Isla Manga

Playa Pedregal

Espíritu Santo

San Andrés

Guerrero

Media Luna

Pozo

Siete

San Antonio

San Juan

Parque del Centenario

Larga

GETSEMANÍ

Arsenal

Plaza de la Independencia

Av del Mercado

Playa de Barahona

Paseo de los Mártires

Bahía de las Ánimas

Muelle de los Pegasos

Gobernador

Av Blas de Lezo

To Bocagrande

Inquisición

Ricaurte   Santo Domi

Upalema

San Juan de Dios

Habanos

Baloco

Vicaría   Damas

Av Santander

See text for key to numbering

N

100 metres
100 yards

Where to stay ⬛
Casa de Pestagua 1 D1
Casa La Fe 2 C2
Casa Marco Polo 3 C3
Casa Viena 4 D4
El Marqués 5 D1
El Viajero 12 D2

El Viajero Hostel 14 C3
Familiar 6 D4
Holiday 7 D4
Hostal Baluarte 8 D4
Hostal La Casona 9 D4
Hostal San Diego 10 B3
Hostal Santa Clara 18 B3

Hostal Santo
Domingo 11 D1
La Passion 15 D2
Las Tres Banderas 16 B3
Marlin 13 D4
Monterrey 17 D3
Villa Colonial 19 D4

Restaurants 🍴
Balkoon 20 B3
Bistro 21 D2
Café Havana 34 D4
Café Lunático 29 D4
Club de Pesca 22 F4
Donde Olano 23 D1

El Coroncoro 24 D4
Juan del Mar 25 B3
La Casa de Socorro 26 F4
La Cocina de Pepina 28 E3
La Mulata 27 C3
Pizza en el parque 30 C2
Portal de los Dulces 36 D2

Santa Lucía 37 D1
Teriyaki 31 B3
Zebra 32 B3

Bars & clubs 🍷
Café del Mar 33 D1
Casa de la Cerveza 35 F4

Donde Fidel 38 D2
Mister Babilla 39 E3
Quiebra Canto 40 D3
Studio 54 41 E3
Tu Candela 42 D2

Cartagena & Caribbean Coast Cartagena ● 25

Mercado on the other side of which is the **Centro Internacional de Convenciones (6)**. It holds gatherings of up to 4000 people and is frequently used now for local and international conventions. It was built in 1972 on the site of the old colourful market, now banished to the interior part of the city. Although the severe fort-like structure is more or less in keeping with the surrounding historic walls and bastions, not everyone believes this is an improvement. When not in use, ask for a guide to show you around.

Immediately to the north is **Plaza de la Independencia**, with the landscaped **Parque del Centenario** alongside. At right angles to the plaza runs the **Paseo de los Mártires**, flanked by the busts of nine patriots executed in the square on 24 February 1816 by the royalist Pablo Morillo after he had retaken the city.

Inner City

At the western end of the Paseo is a tall clock tower, Torre del Reloj, often used as the symbol of Cartagena. To the left is the **Muelle de los Pegasos** (Muelle Turístico) from where the tourist boats leave. Under the clock tower is the **Puerta del Reloj** and the three arches are the principal entrance to the inner walled city. Inside is the **Plaza de los Coches (7)**. As with almost all the plazas of Cartagena, arcades here offer refuge from the tropical sun. At one time, this plaza was the slave market, and later, it was from here that carriages (*coches*) could be hired for local journeys. On the west side of this plaza is the **Portal de los Dulces**, a favourite meeting place and where you can still buy all manner of local sweets and delicacies. It also has a number of good bars, often quite buzzing even during the day. **Plaza de la Aduana (8)**, with a statue of Columbus in the centre and the **Casa de la Aduana** along the wall, originally the tax office and now part of the city administration as the **Palacio Municipal**. Opposite is the **Casa del Premio Real** which was the residence of the representative of the Spanish King. In the corner of the wall is the **Museo de Arte Moderno** ⓘ *Mon-Sat 0900-1200, 1500-1800, US$3.50*, a collection of the work of modern Colombian artists. There is a museum shop.

Past the museum is the **Convento de San Pedro Claver (9)** ⓘ *Mon-Fri 0800-1730, Sat 0800-1600 US$3.50*, and the church and monastery of the same name, built by Jesuits in 1603 and later dedicated to San Pedro Claver, a monk in the monastery, who died in 1654 and was canonized 235 years later. He was called *El Esclavo de los Esclavos*, or *El Apóstol de los Negros*: he used to beg from door to door for money to give to the black slaves brought to the city. His body is in an illuminated glass coffin set in the high marble altar, and his cell and the balcony from which he kept watch for slave ships are shown to visitors. There are brightly coloured birds in the small monastery garden. Several upstairs rooms form a museum, with many interesting items linked or unrelated to Pedro Claver. In the pottery room, for example, is the chair used by the Pope on his visit to Cartagena in 1986. In another room there are several old maps, one of which shows the Caribbean maritime boundaries of Colombia, topical in that disputes with Nicaragua over San Andrés still persist in 2011, despite an international court ruling in favour of Colombia.

Following the wall round, it is well worthwhile climbing up the **Baluarte San Francisco Javier (10)** for a good view of the city and the Caribbean. There is a **Museo Naval del Caribe** ⓘ *Tue-Sun 1000-1700, US$3*, with maps, models and displays of armaments, near the Baluarte. On the corner of Calle Ricaurte is the convent of **Santa Teresa (11)**, founded in 1609 by a rich benefactor as a convent for Carmelite nuns. It had various uses subsequently, as a prison, a military barracks, a school and in the 1970s, was occupied by the police. It was recently purchased by the Banco Central as a heritage investment and has now been converted into a hotel. It is possible to visit the public areas of the hotel and admire the tasteful work of restoration. There is a great view from the roof.

El Bodegón de la Candelaria (12) ① *C Las Damas No 64*, was an elegant colonial residence. It has been faithfully restored and there is some fine panelling and period furniture to see. It is now a restaurant specializing in good seafood. A small shrine in one of the rooms marks the place where the Virgin appeared to a priest who was living there at the time. One block away is **Plaza de Bolívar (13)** with an equestrian statue of the Liberator in the centre. Formerly it was the Plaza de la Inquisición, with the Palacio de la Inquisición (see below), on its west side. The gardens of the plaza were given a face-lift in 2000 and is now an attractive corner of Cartagena.

On the opposite side of the Plaza de Bolívar to the Palacio de la Inquisición is the **Museo del Oro Zenú (14)** ① *Tue-Sat 1000-1300, 1500-1800 free*. Gold and pottery are very well displayed. Specially featured is the Zenú area to the south of Cartagena in the marshlands of the Sinú, San Jorge and Magdalena rivers, which is flooded by the river waters six to eight months of the year. Early drainage systems are featured, as is the advanced level of weaving techniques using the *cañafleche* and other fresh water reeds. This area was densely populated between the second and 10th centuries during which time the gold working skills of the people were developed to the high level that can still be seen today at Mompós, at the northern edge of the Zenú region.

The **Palacio de La Inquisición (15)** ① *Mon-Sat 0800-1800, Sun 1000-1600, US$6*, is on the other side of the Plaza Bolívar. The jurisdiction of this tribunal extended to Venezuela and Panama, and at least 800 were sentenced to death here. There is a small window overlooking the plaza where the public were informed of the sentences. The Palacio houses a modest historical museum, though some of the exhibits are in poor condition. Of special interest are the model of Cartagena in 1808, copies of Alexander Von Humboldt's maps showing the link he discovered between the Orinoco and Amazon rivers (*Canal de Casiquiare*) and of the Maypures rapids on the Orinoco – note that the longitude lines on the maps are west of Paris not Greenwich. The main attraction is the grisly collection of torture instruments. Historical books are on sale at the entrance.

The **Cathedral (16)**, in the northeast corner of Plaza de Bolívar, begun in 1575, was partially destroyed by Francis Drake. Reconstruction was finished by 1612. Great alterations were made between 1912 and 1923. It has a severe exterior, with a fine doorway, and a simply decorated interior. See the gilded 18th-century altar, the Carrara marble pulpit and the elegant arcades which sustain the central nave. Although established in 1610, the present building dates from 1706 with modifications up to 1770. The stone entrance with its coats of arms is well preserved and the ornate wooden door is very notable. The whole building, with its balconies, cloisters and patios, is a fine example of colonial baroque.

Across the street is the **Palacio de la Proclamación** named for the declaration of Independence of the State of Cartagena in November 1811. Before that it was the local Governor's residence, and later where Simón Bolívar stayed in 1826. The building was restored in 1950. The adjacent plaza has interesting local art and sculpture on display daily in high season.

The church and monastery of **Santo Domingo (17)**, built 1570 to 1579 is now a seminary. The old monastery was replaced by the present one in the 17th century. Inside, a miracle-making image of Christ, carved towards the end of the 16th century, is set on a baroque 19th-century altar. This is a most interesting neighbourhood, where very little has changed since the 16th century. In Calle Santo Domingo, No 33-29, is one of the great patrician houses of Cartagena, the **Casa de los Condes de Pestagua**, until recently the Colegio del Sagrado Corazón de Jesús, now a boutique hotel (see page 31). It has a fine colonnaded courtyard, marble floors and magnificent palm trees in the centre garden. Beside the church is the **Plaza de Santo Domingo**, one of the favourite corners of Cartagena, with popular restaurants, bars and cafés. A sculpture by Fernando Botero *La Gorda* is in the Plaza.

North of Santo Domingo at Calle de la Factoría 36-57 is the magnificent **Casa del Marqués de Valdehoyos (18)**, originally owned by the Marqués, who had the lucrative licences to import slaves and flour. The woodcarving is some of the best in Cartagena and the ceilings, chandeliers, wooden arches and balustrading are unique. The views of the city from the fine upper floor balconies are also recommended. Sadly it's been closed for renovations for over a year and a half and wasn't open to the public at the time of writing.

A short walk north is the plaza, church and convent of **La Merced (19)**, founded 1618. The convent, a prison during Morillo's reign of terror, is now occupied by a private university (Jorge Tadeo Lozano), and its church has become the **Teatro Heredia**, which has been beautifully restored.

Two blocks east is Calle de la Universidad, at the end of which is the monastery of **San Agustín (20)**, built in 1580, currently the Universidad de Cartagena. From its chapel, now occupied by a printing press, the pirate Baron de Pointis stole a 500-pound silver sepulchre. It was returned by the King of France but the citizens melted it down to pay their troops during the siege by Morillo in 1815.

One block along Calle de San Agustín is **La Casa Museo de Simón Bolívar (21)**, a collection of memorabilia in the first Cartagena house he stayed in, now the **Biblioteca Bartolomé Calvo** owned by the Banco de la República.

One block along Badillo (Carrera 7) is the church of **Santo Toribio de Mongrovejo (22)** ① *opens for Mass Mon-Fri 0630, 1200, 1815, Sat 0630, 1200, 1800 and Sun 0800, 1000, 1800, 1900, closed at other times*. Building began in 1729. In 1741, during Admiral Vernon's siege, a cannon ball fell into the church during Mass and lodged in one of the central columns; the ball is now in a recess in the west wall. The font of Carrara marble in the Sacristy is a masterpiece. There is a beautiful carved ceiling (*mudéjar* style) above the main altar with a rear lighted figure of Christ.

The church and monastery of **Santa Clara de Assisi (23)** is close by. It was built 1617-1621, and has been spectacularly restored. It is now a hotel, but this is one you must see. Behind the hotel is the orange **Casa de Gabriel García Márquez (24)**, the most famous living Colombian author, on the corner of Calle del Curato.

Beyond the Santa Clara is the **Plaza de Las Bóvedas (25)**. Towards the sea, before Las Bóvedas, you will see a bank (*espiga*) leading to a jetty used in colonial times when the water came up to the walls, as shown on the 1808 map displayed in the **Palacio de la Inquisición**. All the land below the walls has since been reclaimed, with sports fields, recreational areas and the Avenida Santander/Paseo de la Muralla, a busy bypass to the city. The walls of Las Bóvedas, built 1799, are 12 m high and from 15- to 18-m thick. At the base of the wall are 23 dungeons, now containing tourist shops. Both an illuminated underground passage and a drawbridge lead from Las Bóvedas to the fortress of La Tenaza, which guarded the approach to the city from the coast to the northeast.

Casa de Núñez (26) ① *Mon-Sat 0800-1200, 1400-1800, US$0.50, there is also a monument to the 1886 constitution in the small park beside the lagoon*, just outside the walls of La Tenaza in El Cabrero district was the home of Rafael Núñez, four-time president of Colombia. He established the constitution of 1886 and wrote the national anthem. His grandiose marble tomb is in the delightful small **Ermita El Cabrero** church opposite.

Back along the lagoon is the old **Plaza de Toros (27)**, bull ring. It is an interesting wooden building but now abandoned and in a dangerous state. It cannot be visited.

Closer to the centre, where the main road leads into the city, is a roundabout, in the centre of which is the monument to **La India Catalina (28)**, Pedro de Heredia's indigenous interpreter in the early days of the Spanish conquest. A miniature of this statue is given to the winner of the annual Cartagena film festival – a Colombian 'Oscar'.

The ramparts

In addition to being a spectacular feature of Cartagena, the city walls make a great walk and are an excellent way to visit many of the attractions inside. A good place to start is the **Baluarte San Francisco Javier (10)** from where, with a few ups and downs, it is continuous to **La India Catalina (28)**. From this point, there are two further sections along the lagoons to the **Puente Román (1)**. The final section along the Calle del Arsenal can be completed through the **Playa de Barahona**, a bayside park, which is busy at weekends. The entire walk takes about 1½ hours, although if you take a camera it can take considerably longer. It is a spectacular walk in the morning around 0600 and equally at sunset. At many points you can drop down to see the sights detailed above in the tour of the old city.

Three of Cartagena's sights are off our map. Two of them, the Fortress of San Fernando and the Castillo San Felipe de Barajas, across the **Puente Heredia (3)** have been described above. The third is **Convento La Popa** ① *daily 0845-1730, US$3.50, children and students US$2, guides available*, on La Popa hill, nearly 150 m high, from where there is a fine view of the harbour and the city. It is not recommended to walk up on your own; either take a guided tour or take a public bus to Teatro Miramar at the foot of the hill (US$0.50), then bargain for a taxi up, about US$7 return. If driving, take Carrera 21 off Avenida Pedro de Heredia, and follow the winding road to the top. The Augustinian church and monastery of Santa Cruz (Convento La Popa), and restored ruins of the convent dating from 1608 can be found here. In the church is the beautiful little image with a golden crown of the Virgin of La Candelaria, reputed as a deliverer from plague and a protector against pirates. The statue was blessed by the Pope on his visit in 1986. The Virgin's day is 2 February and for nine days before the feast thousands of people go up the hill by car, on foot, or on horseback. On the day itself people carry lighted candles as they go up the hill. There is an attractive bougainvillea-covered cloister with a well in the centre, and a museum with illuminated manuscripts, old maps, music books, relics and an image of the *Cabro de Oro* (golden goat) found by the Augustinians on the site, presumed to be an object of veneration of the indigenous people who previously inhabited the area. The name was bestowed on the hill because of an imagined likeness to a ship's poop deck.

Beaches

Take a bus south from the Puerta del Reloj, taxi US$2.50, or walk to **Bocagrande**, where the beaches can be dirty in parts and often crowded. You will also be constantly hassled. The sea is a little dirty, though better if you go as far as the Hilton at the end of the peninsula.

Marbella beach is an alternative, just north of Las Bóvedas. This is the locals' beach, and therefore quieter than Bocagrande during the week and good for swimming, though subject at times to dangerous currents.

The **Bocachica** beach, on Tierrabomba island, isn't very clean either, and you may be hassled here too. Boats leave for Bocachica from Muelle Turístico. The departure point is the two-storey glass building halfway along, which also has some tourist information. The round trip can take up to two hours each way and costs about US$2.50 with the regular service, more if with private boats. *Ferry Dancing*, about half the price of the faster, luxury boats, carries dancing passengers. Boats taking in Bocachica and the San Fernando fortress include *Alcatraz*, which runs a daily trip from the Muelle Turístico. Alternatively, you can cross from Bocagrande; *lanchas* leave from near the Hilton Hotel and go to Punta Arena beach on Tierrabomba.

Boats to the Islas del Rosario (see page 39) may stop at the **San Fernando** fortress on Tierrabomba island and **Playa Blanca** on the Isla de Barú for one hour. You can bargain with the boatman to collect you later. Take food and water since these are expensive on the island. Barú, a long thin island, has mostly fine white-sand beaches which are slowly being exploited by upmarket hotel complexes that will hopefully respect this fragile environment. The stopping place for tourist boats from Cartagena is Playa Blanca which is crowded in the mornings, but peaceful after the tour boats have left at around 1400. There have been reports of people drinking alcohol and then renting jetskis at Playa Blanca; keep your wits about you when swimming or snorkelling, as safety measures aren't always complied with.

Another alternative is to catch a fishing boat from the Mercado Bazurto (a short distance beyond La Popa) to Playa Blanca, leaving around 0830, US$10-12 one way, and take another one back when you choose, although this might not be on the same day and they only leave when full. Note that this is not a legal practice and sometimes there are police checks. Many consider this to be the best beach in the region, with stretches of white sand and shady palm groves. There are several simple and cheap places to stay here and **Mama Root** is highly recommended. Other places include **Hugo's Place**, which has a campsite, restaurant and hires hammocks with mosquito nets, and **El Paraíso**. The **Wintenberg Camp** has good *cabañas*. Remember to take water, as there is little on the island. You can also reach Playa Blanca by taking the bus to Pasacaballo, crossing the Canal del Dique by canoe and continuing by truck or jeep to the beach. If walking, allow 2½ hours in all. If staying the night at Playa Blanca in *cabañas* or tents, beware of ferocious sandflies. A *cabaña* will typically cost about US$12 per night. **Note** Pay for boat trips on board if possible, and be certain that you and the operator understands what you are paying for.

The little fishing village of **La Boquilla**, northeast of Cartagena, is near the end of a sandy promontory between the Ciénaga de Tesca and the Caribbean, about 20 minutes past the airport. There's a camping area with an attractive pool surrounded by palm trees, entrance US$2. A good beach nearby, El Paraíso, is busy at weekends but quiet during the week; good fish dishes available. Visit the mangrove swamps nearby to see the birds.

For sleeping and eating price codes and other relevant information, see pages 8-13.

● Where to stay

Hotel prices rise for the high season, Nov-Mar, and Jun-Jul. From 15 Dec to 31 Jan they can rise by as much as 50% on Bocagrande beach; in town you will find not find much below US$20. Hotels tend to be heavily booked right through to Mar.

Around the old city *p23, map p24*

Getsemaní and La Matuna
Many cheap hotels on C Media Luna used to be brothels, but the area has cleaned up its act and now has lots of good budget options and new eateries.
$$$ Monterrey, Paseo de los Mártires, Cra 8B, No 25-103, T650 3030, www.hotel monterrey.com.co. Just outside the old city walls and with a view onto the Puerta del Reloj, this hotel has rooms in simple colours with balconies, TV and hot water. It also has a sunroof with a jacuzzi and access to internet.
$$-$ Hostal Baluarte, Media Luna, No 10-81, T664 2208. A family-run, converted colonial house with a fine courtyard shaded by a mango tree and wrought-iron furniture, rocking chairs and hammocks in which to relax. Can arrange tours to the Islas del Rosario and has laundry service. Rooms a little small.
$ Casa Viena, C San Andrés, No 30-53, T664 6242, www.casaviena.com. A hub of informa-tion on activities in Cartagena, this hostel in Getsemaní is very popular with backpackers. Offers internet access, use of a kitchen, washing machine, a TV room and very cheap dormitories. Bustling and busy, good value.
$ Casa Villa Colonial, C de la Media Luna No 10-89, T664 5421, www.casavilla colonial.com. Set around a lovely courtyard, this is a family-run hotel with a/c, TV, free

internet in the lobby and breakfast available for a charge. Also has a sister hotel, **Hotel Villa Colonial** in C de las Maravillas.
$ Familiar, C del Guerrero, No 29-66, off Media Luna, T664 2464. Fresh and bright, family-run hotel with rooms set around a colonnaded patio. Has a good noticeboard full of information, a laundry service and use of a kitchen. Friendly and recommended.
$ Holiday, C de la Media Luna, No 10-47, T664 0948, www.hostelholidaycaribe.com. Rooms and dorms open on to a corridor patio with potted plants and tables. There's a small kitchen and a good information board. Internet access and free coffee.
$ Hostal La Casona, C Tripita y Media, Cra 10, No 31-32, T/F664 1301, www.la casonahostel.com. Has a breezy central courtyard and rooms with private bath. Laundry service provided.
$ Hotel Marlin, C de la Media Luna, No 10-35, T664 3507, www.hotelmarlincartagena.com. Aquatic-themed hostel run by a friendly Colombian. Has fine balcony looking onto the busy C de la Media Luna. Laundry service, free coffee, internet access, lockers, tours and bus tickets organized. Breakfast included. Recommended.

El Centro and San Diego
$$$$ Casa de Pestagua, C Santo Domingo, No 33-63, T664 9510, www.casapestagua. com. Formerly home to the Conde de Pestagua, this historic house has been restored by architect Alvaro Barrera Herrera with great care. From the street it opens up into a magnificent colonnaded courtyard lined with enormous palm trees. Beyond is a swimming pool and spa, and on the top floor a sun terrace with jacuzzi and sea views. Also has Wi-Fi.
$$$$ El Marqués, C Nuestra Señora del Carmen, No 33-41, T664 7800, www.elmarqueshotel boutique.com.

Another house belonging to the Pestagua family. The central courtyard, dominated by a large crumbling wall of draping ivy, features giant birdcages, hanging bells and large palm trees. The rooms are crisp, white and have Wi-Fi and iPod docks. Recent additions to the hotel include a Peruvian restaurant, a wine cellar and spa. Exquisite.

$$$$ La Passion, C Estanco del Tabaco, No 35-81, T664 8605, www.lapassionhotel.com. In the heart of the old city, this grand building brings the concept of the Marrakech boutique hotel to Latin America. Its French owners have trawled the globe in search of exquisite furnishings. A mixture of colonial and Republican-era architecture, **La Passion** has cathedral-like rooms that provide modern, elegant and discreet comfort in the shape of plasma TVs, Wi-Fi and MP3 players. Breakfast is included in the price and served on the sublime roof terrace, next to the swimming pool. Also offers spa treatments including different massage and boat trips to nearby Islas del Rosario. Highly recommended.

$$$$ Santa Clara, Calle del Torno, No 39-29, T650 4700, www.sofitel.com. The French Sofitel group own this magnificently restored early 17th-century convent on the enchanting Plaza de San Diego. Rooms, however, are in a modern annex and most have a balcony looking onto a large swimming pool, invariably with views of the sea. Has 2 restaurants, a bar and a spa.

$$$$-$$$ Casa La Fe, Parque Fernández de Madrid, C 2a de Badillo, No 36-125, T664 0306, www.casalafe.com. A Republican-era house (c1930) on the delightful Parque Fernández de Madrid, the 14 en suite bedrooms of Casa La Fe have been restored by a British-Colombian team. It has a pool-jacuzzi on the roof and other services such as Wi-Fi, free bicycle use, and free breakfast served in a leafy patio. Organizes tours.

$$$ Casa Marco Polo, C de los Siete Infantes, No 9-89, T316-874 9478, cantolindo1@hotmail.com. Private rooms in a 450-year-old colonial mansion belonging to a local *cumbia* musician. 2 rooms, 1 cheaper (**$$**), have a/c, cable TV and share a roof terrace with stunning views of Barrio San Diego. Breakfast included and limited use of kitchen possible. Highly recommended.

$$$ Hostal San Diego, C de las Bóvedas, No 39-120, T660 1433, www.hostal sandiego.com. Near the delightful Plaza San Diego, this colonial building with its salmon pink exterior has modern rooms which open out onto a tiled courtyard. A/c and Wi-Fi.

$$$ Las Tres Banderas, C Cochera de Hobo, No 38-66, T660 0160, www.hotel3 banderas.com. Another hotel in the bohemian district of San Diego, this old building is split over 2 breezy courtyards with water features. All rooms have a safe and come with breakfast included. Free internet access. Also offers massage treatments.

$$ Hostal Santo Domingo, C Santo Domingo, No 33-46, T664 2268, hsantodomingopiret@ yahoo.es. If you are looking for a budget option in the old town, this is one of your best bets. Rooms are simple but clean and open up on to a sunny patio. Breakfast is included, there is a laundry service, free Wi-Fi and the gate is usually locked, so security is good.

$$ Hotel El Viajero, C del Porvenir, No 35-68, piso 2, T664 3289, hotelviajero664@ hotmail.com, www.hotelelviajero.com. Ideally located in the centre of the old town, this 2nd floor hostel is more practical than attractive. Organizes tours, has a/c, TV, Wi-Fi and access to a kitchen.

$$-$ El Viajero Hostel, C de los Siete Infantes 9-45, T660 2598, www.elviajero hostels.com. New spacious hostel with private rooms and dorms. A/c in every room, breakfast included, free Wi-Fi and bar. Busy and popular, but a bit noisy.

Beaches *p30*

Bocagrande

$$$$ Capilla del Mar, Cra 1 No 8-12, T018000-510077 or 650 1500, www.capilla delmar.com. Resort hotel across the road from the beach, with swimming pool on top floor and 3 restaurants serving seafood and *parrillas*.

$$$$ Hotel Almirante, Av San Martín, C 6 esq, T655 4700, www.hotelesestelar.com. Popular with affluent Colombian tourists, this high-rise hotel has 250 rooms and all the usual resort facilities, including a half moon-shaped pool on the top floor with good views out over the beaches.

$$$$ Hotel Caribe, Cra 1, No 2-87, T650 1160, www.hotelcaribe.com. Enormous Caribbean-style hotel with 2 newer annexes, a/c, beautiful grounds and a swimming pool in the expensive restaurant. Has several bars overlooking the sea.

$$$ Bahía, Cra 4 with C 4, T665 0316, www.hotelbahiacartagena.com. Has the feel of a 1950s hotel. Discreet, quiet, with fine pool and restaurant.

$$$ Hotel Charlotte, Av San Martín, No 7-126, T665 9201, www.hotelescharlotte. com. Stylishly designed in cool whites. Has a pool, and Wi-Fi in the lobby. Smart restaurant serves up Italian food. Recommended.

$$$ Playa Club, Av San Martín, No 4-87, T665 0552, www.hotelplayaclubcartagena. com. Some of the rooms are painted in lurid colours but are otherwise fine and it has an inviting pool and direct access to the beach. TV, a/c and breakfast included.

$$ Casa Grande, Av del Malecón, No 9-128, T665 6806. Yellow and blue house set back from the beach with spacious rooms off a tranquil garden at the back. Recommended.

$$ Ibatama, Av San Martín 7-46, T665 1127, hotelesibatamactg@yahoo.com. Has a pleasant terrace looking out over 1 of the principal streets, with a/c and TV, though the rooms are quite small and few have windows.

$$ Leonela, Cra 3, 7-142, T665 4761, www.hostaleonela.com. A very helpful and friendly couple have run this hotel for more than 30 years. Has a family atmosphere and a small restaurant serving breakfast. Also has money exchange.

$$ Mary, No 6-53, T6652833. Basic rooms but pleasant and friendly. A/c or fan.

🍴 Restaurants

At cafés try *patacón*, a round flat 'cake' made of green banana, mashed and baked; also from street stalls in Parque del Centenario in the early morning. At restaurants ask for *sancocho* the local soup of the day of vegetables and fish or meat. Also try *obleas* for a snack, biscuits with jam, cream cheese or caramel fudge (*arequipe*), and *buñuelos*, deep-fried cheese dough balls. Fruit juices are fresh, tasty and cheap in Cartagena: a good place is on the Paseo de los Pegasos (Av Blas de Lezo) from the many stalls alongside the boats.

The city's fortifications *p22*
$$$ Club de Pesca, San Sebastián de Pastelillo fort, Manga Island, T660 4594, www.clubde pesca.com. Wonderful setting, perhaps the most famous fish and seafood restaurant in Cartagena, though expensive. Warmly recommended.

Around the old city *p23, map p24*

Getsemaní and La Matuna

With spiralling property prices Getsemaní is undergoing the same gentrification treatment as Centro and San Diego, evidenced by an increasing number of smart restaurants that have opened up in the area.

$$-$ La Casa de Socorro, C Larga, No 8B-112, T664 4658. This seafood restaurant is popular with locals and does very good *bandejas de pescado* and *arroz con camarones*. Take note that there are 2 rival restaurants of the same name on the same street. This one is the original and better. Friendly and recommended.

$$-$ La Cocina de Pepina, Callejón Vargas, No 9A-6. A new restaurant serving Colombian Caribbean cuisine, run by established chef and cookbook author María Josefina Yances Guerra.

$ Café Havana, C de la Media Luna y C del Guerrero, www.cafehavanacartagena.com. A fantastic Cuban bar and restaurant, which feels like it has been transported from Havana brick by brick. The walls are festooned with black-and-white portraits of Cuban salsa stars and it has live bands playing most nights. Note that it doesn't take credit cards. Highly recommended.

$ Café Lunático, C Media Luna 10-89 (next door to **Hostal Baluarte**). Interesting café with fresh juices, local and Indian dishes. Also sells weavings and blankets.

$ El Coroncoro, C Tripita y Media, No 31-28. More typical of the area, very popular at lunchtime with locals. It's atmospheric and offers *menús del día* from US$3.

El Centro and San Diego

Plaza San Diego has several good restaurants serving up a variety of international cuisines.

$$$ Santa Lucía, C Santo Domingo 3-30, piso 2. Lovely Argentine-style parrilla restaurant overlooking bustling Plaza Santo Domingo. Steaks to die for and generous portions. Highly recommended.

$$$-$$ Donde Olano, C Santo Domingo with Inquisición. Art deco restaurant serving French and Creole cuisine in a cosy atmosphere. Try their fantastic seafood platter, Tentaciones de Zeus. Well worth the price.

$$ Juan del Mar, Plaza San Diego, No 8-18. Offers 2 restaurants in 1: inside serves expensive seafood while outside cooks up fine, thin-based pizzas, though you are likely to be harassed by street hawkers.

$$ Teriyaki, Plaza San Diego, No 8-28. Next to **Zebra**, serves sushi and Thai food in smart surroundings.

$$ Zebra, Plaza San Diego, No 8-34. Café with wide selection of coffees, hot sandwiches and African dishes.

$$-$ Bistro, C de los Ayos, No 4-46. German-run restaurant with a relaxed atmosphere. Sofas, music, European menu at reasonable prices. Has a German bakery and tasty food. Closed Sun. Recommended.

$$-$ La Mulata, C Quero, No 9-58. A popular lunchtime venue with locals, you get a selection of set menu dishes. Try the excellent seafood casserole and coconut lemonade. Has Wi-Fi.

$ Balkoon, C de Tumbamuertos, No 38-85, Piso 2. Small restaurant overlooking the Plaza de San Diego. Great views and nice atmosphere.

$ Pizza en el parque, C 2a de Badillo, No 36-153. This small kiosk serves up delicious pizzas with some interesting flavours (pear and apple) which you can munch on while enjoying the delightful atmosphere of Parque Fernández Madrid.

The beaches *p30*
There are good fish dishes in La Boquilla.

Bocagrande

$$ Carbón de Palo, Av San Martín, No 6-40. Steak heaven, cooked on an outdoor *parrilla*.

$$ Restaurante Arabe, Cra 3A, No 8-83, T665 4365. Upmarket Arab restaurant serving tagines, etc. A/c, indoor seating or pleasant outdoor garden.

$ Jeno's, Av San Martín, No 7-162. Eat in or take away pizza.

$ Juan Valdez Café, Av San Martín, No 7-17, Starbucks-style chain serving various types of coffee and sandwiches. Has Wi-Fi.

$ La Fonda Antioqueña, Cra 2, No 6-164. Traditional Colombian, nice atmosphere.

$ Ranchería's, Av 1A, No 8-86. Serves seafood and meats in thatched huts just off the beach. *Menú del día*, US$8.

🍸 Bars and clubs

Cartagena boasts a lively dance scene and the atmosphere in the city after dark is addictive. Any one of the cafés next to the Santo Domingo church is a great place for a drink.

Around the old city *p23*

Many of the hotels have evening entertainment and can arrange *chiva* (brightly coloured local bus) tours, usually with free drinks and live music on the bus.

There are good local nightclubs in Bocagrande eg **La Escollera**, Cra 1, next to El Pueblito shopping centre, with other places nearby including spontaneous musical groups on or near the beach most evenings.

Most places don't get going until after 2400, though the Cuban bar **Donde Fidel**, on Portal de los Dulces, and **Café Havana**, on C de la Media Luna in Getsemaní start a little earlier and are highly recommended if you want to hear Cuban salsa. The former is open daytime and the atmosphere is good even early on. C del Arsenal hosts the majority of Cartagena's clubs and you will probably wind up there if you are really giving the city's nightlife a go. Most bars play crossover music.

Café del Mar, on Baluarte de Santo Domingo, El Centro. The place to go at sundown, where surrounded by ancient canons you can watch the sun set over the bay. Highly recommended, but very popular. Get here early to get a seat for the sundowners.

Casa de la Cerveza, at the end of C del Arsenal. Low sofas peppered around the battlements.

Mister Babilla, C del Arsenal. The most popular and exclusive bar. Take something warm with you – they really like to blast the a/c here.

Quiebra Canto, C Media Luna at Parque Centenario, next to **Hotel Monterrey**, Getsemaní. The best place for salsa. Nice atmosphere, free admission.

Tu Candela, Portal de los Dulces, next door to Donde Fidel Open from 2000.

Gay bars
Studio 54, C Larga, No 24, Getsemaní.

🎭 Entertainment

Cartagena *p20, map p24*

Cinema
There are many cinemas in Cartagena. In Bocagrande there is one in the **Centro Commercial Bocagrande**. Others are in the **Centro Comercial Paseo de la Castellana** on Av Pedro de Heredia and in **Centro Comercial La Plazuela** in the same area. **Teatro Heredia**, has been beautifully restored.

Dance
El Colegio del Cuerpo, C Larga, No 10-27, T664 3184, www.elcolegiodelcuerpo.org. A classical dance studio that works with children from Cartagena's slums. They perform internationally and occasionally in Cartagena.

🎉 Festivals

Cartagena *p20, map p24*
End-Jan Hay Festival Cartagena, www.hay festival.com. Franchise of the famous literary festival in the UK, takes place at the end of the month, with internationally renowned writers.
Jan-Feb La Candelaria (Candelmas).
Feb-Mar International Film Festival, Beluarte San Francisco, C San Juan de Dios, T660 1701/2, www.ficcifestival.com. The longest running festival of its kind in Latin America. Although mainly Spanish American films are featured, the US, Canada and European countries are represented in the week-long showings.
1 Jun celebrations commemorating the Foundation of Cartagena.
Nov Independencia. In the 2nd week of the month, to celebrate the Independence of Cartagena. People in masks and fancy dress

dance in the streets. There are beauty contests, battles of flowers and general mayhem.
Dec Caribbean Music Festival. Groups from all over the Caribbean region and beyond perform salsa, reggae, etc.

○ Shopping

Cartagena *p20, map p24*

There is a good selection of *artesanías* at **Compendium** on Plaza Bolívar. **Galería Cano** (www.galeriacano.com.co), next to the Gold Museum has excellent reproductions of pre-Columbian designs. Pricey antiques can be bought in C Santo Domingo and there are a number of jewellery shops near Plaza de Bolívar in Centro, which specialize in emeralds. Beware of 'Cuban cigars' sold on the street; **Habanos**, C San Juan de Dios, has a wide selection but in general you will pay less in Bogotá.

The handicraft shops in the Plaza de las Bóvedas (**25**) have the best selection in town but tend to be expensive – cruise ship passengers are brought here. Woollen *blusas* are good value; try the **Tropicano** in Pierino Gallo building in Bocagrande. Also in this building are reputable jewellery shops. **Abaco**, C de la Iglesia with C Mantilla, No 3-86, www.abacolibros.com. A bookshop, which is a popular hangout for local writers and poets. Delightful atmosphere and a café serving juices and snacks.
Centro Comercial Getsemaní, C Larga between San Juan and Plaza de la Independencia. A large shopping centre. Good *artesanías* in the grounds of the convent.
H Stern, Pierino Gallo shopping centre and at the **Hilton Hotel**. Jewellery shop.
Instituto Geográfico Agustín Codazzi, C 34, No 3A-31, Edificio Inurbe, www.igac.gov.co. Maps.
Librería Nacional, C 2 (Badillo), No 36-27, T664 1448,www.librerianacional.com. Bookshop.

Magali París, Av Venezuela y C del Boquete. A supermarket, with a/c and cafeteria.
Santo Domingo, C Santo Domingo, No 3-34. Recommended for jewellery.
Upalema, C San Juan de Dios, No 3-99. A good selection of handicrafts.

Markets
The main market is to the southeast of the old city near La Popa off Av Pedro de Heredia (**Mercado Bazurto**). Good bargains in the **La Matuna** market, open daily including Sun.

▲ What to do

Cartagena *p20, map p24*

Diving
La Tortuga Dive Shop, Edif Marina del Rey, C 1 2 23, Local 4, Av del Retorno, Bocagrande, T665 6995, www.tortugadive.com. A minicourse with 2 dives costs US$105. A faster boat, which allows trips to Isla Barú as well as Los Rosarios.
Diving Planet, C Estanco del Aguardiente, No 5-94, T664 2171, www.divingplanet.org. PADI open certificate course, PADI e-learning, snorkelling trips, English spoken. Associated hotel in Cartagena, **Puertas de Cartagena**, www.hotelpuertasdecartagena.com.

Football
Estadio de Futbol Pedro de Heredia, Villa Olímpica, south of the city. Games are infrequent. Seats for matches cost between US$5 and US$13.50.

Horse-drawn carriage rides
Horse-drawn carriages can be hired for for a trip around the walled city from Puerta del Reloj, about US$16 for up to 4 people. Or from opposite Hotel El Dorado, Av San Martín, in Bocagrande, to ride into town at night (romantic but a rather short ride).

Tour operators
Aventure Colombia, C del Santísimo, No 8-55, T664 8500, T314-588 2378 (mob), www.aventurecolombia.com. The only tour organizer of its kind in Cartagena, Frenchman Mathieu Perrot-Bohringer and his Colombian wife Angélica specialize in alternative tours across Colombia, focusing on trekking, eco-tourism and rural tourism. They aim to practice responsible tourism, working (wherever possible) with local and indigenous groups. For further information on boat trips they organize, see Transport, page 38. Highly recommended.

Ocean & Land, Cra 2, No 4-15, Edificio Antillas, Bocagrande, T665 7772, oceanland tours@yahoo.com. Organizes city tours, rumbas in *chivas* (brightly coloured local buses) and other local activities.

Yachting
Club Náutico, Av Miramar No 19-50, on Manga Island across the Puente Román, T660 4863, www.clubnauticocartagena.com. Good for opportunities to charter, crew or for finding a lift to other parts of the Caribbean.

☺ Transport

Cartagena *p20, map p24*

Air
Direct flights daily to major Colombian cities and to smaller places in the north of the country. International flights direct daily to Miami and Panama. From Dec to Mar flights can be overbooked, so best to turn up at the airport early. Daily flights to all main cities and international destinations.

Airline offices Copa Air, Cra 6, No 8-116 (Bocagrade), T6650428; **Avianca**, C del Arzobispado, No 34-52, T6641729, also in Bocagrande, C 7, No 7-17, L 7, T665 5727 and at the airport; **CC Invercredito**, Local 18, T664 9077, Mon-Fri 0800-1800, Sat 0900-1300.

Bus
Colectivos for **Barranquilla** leave from C 70, Barrio Crespo every 2 hrs and cost US$14 and are a good option as they do a centre-to-centre service. There is a regular bus to **Barranquilla**, every 15 mins, 2-3 hrs, US$8, Berlinas del Fonce; Brasilia; Concorde; La Costeña.To **Medellín**, 665 km, approximately 1 every hour starting from 0530, 13-16 hrs, US$60, **Brasilia; Copetran; Rápido Ochoa** (slightly cheaper, recommended), book early (2 days in advance at holiday times). The road is now paved throughout, but in poor condition. To **Santa Marta**, 1 every hour, 4 hrs, US$13.50, **Berlinas del Fonce; Brasilia; La Costeña.**

To **Bogotá** via Barranquilla and Bucaramanga, 16 a day, 21-28 hrs (depending on number of checkpoints), US$75, with **Berlinas del Fonce** (3 a day); **Brasilia; Concorde; Copetran; Rápido Ochoa.** To **Magangué** on the *Magdalena*, US$12, 4 hrs with **Brasilia.** To **Mompós**, 0700, 12 hrs including ferry crossing from Magangué, US$17, **Unitransco.** To **Riohacha**, US$22. Bus to **Maicao** on Venezuelan frontier, every hour 0500-1200, 2 in the evening, 12 hrs, US$27, with **Brasilia.**

Car hire
Several of the bigger hotels have car rental company offices in their foyers, such as Hotel Bahía, Bocagrande, C 14, No 3-59, local 1. There are several car rental companies in Edif Torremolinos, Av San Martín: **International Car Rentals**, T665 5399; **National**, T665 3336; **Rentacars**, T665 2852. At the airport, try **Platinum** on 2nd floor, T666 4112.

Sea
Intermittent boats go from Cartagena to **Porvenir** in the San Blas Islands (Panama); the journey takes about 2 days and the 1-way fare is US$450-500 per person,

including food and 3 nights touring the San Blas archipelago. The sailboats will normally end in **San Blas** from where you can continue your journey by air or overland to Panama City. The skippers will help with immigration paperwork.

There are 3 boats that provide a regular service between Cartagena and San Blas. Highly recommended is **Stella Luna**, T312-681 7833 (Colombia) or T507-6768 6121 (Panama), captained by Hernando Higuera, a key figure in establishing Cartagena's sailing club, who has strong friendships with many of the indigenous Cuna of San Blas. Also try: **Tango**, run by French skipper David, T314-558 8945 (mob) or German captain Guido, T316-243 6324 (mob), who also owns a backpackers' hostel in Panama. Take your time before choosing a boat. Some captains are irresponsible and unreliable. The journey is cramped and you do not want to make it with a captain you do not get on with.

Aventure Colombia, T314-588 2378 (mob), www.aventurecolombia.com, can provide reliable information on trustworthy boats and skippers. Also organize 8-day tours to San Blas via the Islas del Rosario, Islas de San Bernardo and Sapzurro in the Darién, costing about US$800 per person, including food.

Also try noticeboards at backpacker hotels such as Hotel Casa Viena or ask around at the Yacht Club (Club Nautico). In Panama, the only reliable information is in Porvenir.

Taking a vehicle It is possible to ship a car from Cartagena to Panama. 3 companies that can arrange shipment of vehicles to Panama are: **Agencia Internacional Ltda**, Cra 2, No 9-145, Edif Nautilus, Bocagrande, T664 7539, agents for **King Ocean Services**, 11000 NW 29 St, Suite 201, Doral, FL, T305-591 7595, www.kingocean.com, serving Cartagena, Panama and Miami; **Hermann Schwyn**, Edif Chambacu Business Center, Piso 6, PO Box 1626, T650 3610, www.schwyn.com.

Note On the street, do not be tempted by offers of jobs or passages aboard ship. Jobs should have full documentation from the Seamen's Union office and passages should only be bought at a recognized shipping agency.

Directory

Cartagena *p20, map p24*

Embassies and consulates For your country's embassy or consulates in Colombia, see http://embassy.goabroad.com.
Immigration **DAS**, just beyond Castillo San Felipe, Cra 20B, No 29-18, Plaza de la Ermita (Pie de la Popa), T656 3007, helpful. DAS passport office is in C Gastelbondo, near the ramparts. Get free visa extensions here.
Language The **Nueva Lengua School,** www.nuevalengua. com, offers courses ranging from half-day schedules to a scheme that arranges volunteer jobs. There are even Spanish courses combined with dance, music, adventure, kite-surfing or diving.
Medical services There is a recompression chamber at the naval hospital, Bocagrande; **Hospital Bocagrande**, C 5/Cra 6, Bocagrande, T655 0962, www.hospitalbocagrande.com.co.

Around Cartagena

Cartagena is surrounded on almost all sides by water and travellers will be drawn to the city's sparkling Caribbean coast. Islas del Rosario and Islas San Bernardo are glistening examples of what a tropical paradise should look like, and for those on a budget there is Playa Blanca on the Barú Peninsula. To the northeast of Cartagena, the coastline is characterized by *ciénagas* (mangrove swamps), such as the Ciénaga La Caimanera, which provide plenty of opportunities to observe the wildlife that subsists in these remarkable ecosystems. A few kilometres further on is the Volcán del Totumo, an extraordinary crater-like mud hole where bathers can wallow before washing off in the nearby *ciénaga*.

Volcán del Totumo

Along the coast north of Cartagena, at La Boquilla, is the Ciénaga la Caimanera, a labyrinth of mangrove swamps full of wildlife. Canoe trips can be made to explore these (motorboats are not allowed). Local guides cost US$10 per person, and they will catch oysters for you to eat. Further north is **Galerazamba**, there is no accommodation but good local food. Nearby are the clay baths of **Volcán del Totumo** ⓘ *entry to the cone US$2.50 adults, US$1.75 children, the unusual experience will cost you US$2 and you wash off in the nearby Ciénaga*, in beautiful surroundings. Climb up steep steps to the lip of the 20-m-high crater and slip into the grey cauldron of mud, about 10 m across, at a comfortable temperature and reputed to be over 500 m deep. Massages are available for a small extra fee. You can catch a bus from Cartagena to Galerazamba at the Mercado Popular, Carerra 2 with Calle 16 (US$1.50, two hours), ask to be dropped off at Lomo Arena where the bus turns off to Galerazamba. Walk along the main road for 2 km to a right turn signposted to Volcán del Totumo which is 1.5 km along a poor road. Hitching is possible. Taking a tour from Cartagena will cost more but will save a lot of time. **Aventure Colombia** ⓘ *C del Santísimo, No 8-55, Cartagena, T664 8500 or T314-588 2378 (mob), www.aventurecolombia.com*, organizes tours to the volcano for US$28, including transport and lunch at La Boquilla or Playa de Manzanillo. A tour of both the volcano and the mangroves is US$42.

Islas del Rosario → For listings, see pages 46-51.

The National Park of Corales del Rosario and San Bernardo embraces the archipelago of Rosario (a group of 30 coral islets, 45 km southwest of the Bay of Cartagena) and the mangrove coast of the long island of Barú to its furthest tip. **Isla Grande** and some of the smaller islets are easily accessible by day trippers and those who wish to stay in one of the hotels. Permits are needed for the rest, entrance fee US$6. These picture-postcard islands, low lying and densely vegetated, with narrow strips of fine sand beaches, form part of a coral reef. **Rosario** (the largest and best conserved) and **Tesoro** both have small lakes, some of which connect to the sea, and many of the smaller islets are privately owned. There is a profusion of aquatic and birdlife here and the **San Martín de Pajarales Aquarium** (**Oceanario**) ⓘ *US$10*, is worth visiting. Look out for the huge catfish but note that the price of entry is not included in boat fares. The island has access to some of the best coral reefs in the archipelago and diving and snorkelling are available. The **Hotel El Caribe** in Bocagrande

Mud volcanoes

The Caribbean coast is peppered with several geological curiosities popularly known as 'mud volcanoes'. These large mud pools are believed to be the result of underground oil and gas deposits, which combine with water, forcing the mud to ooze to the surface. Often they form conical mounds, hence the name. Many of these pools can be found between the Gulf of Urabá and Santa Marta. Turbo has several in its proximity (Rodosalín, El Alto de Mulatos and Caucal), as does San Pedro de Urabá. The Volcán de Totumo is a popular day trip from Cartagena, but the pick of the bunch is Arboletes, where an enormous 30-m-wide lake has formed a stone's throw from the beach.

Wallowing in the grey-black mud is a strange experience. It's impossible to sink and attempts to swim are about as worthwhile as trying to battle your way across a vat of treacle. When you have had enough, clamber out and join the line of mud-caked figures waddling down to the Caribbean for a wash and a swim. The stuff is reportedly an excellent exfoliant and does wonders for the skin and hair.

(see page 33) offers scuba lessons in its pool followed by diving at its resort on Isla Grande, for US$230 and upwards. ▸▸ *For further diving information, see What to do, page 50.*

Travel agencies and the hotels offer excursions from the Muelle Turístico, leaving 0700-0900 and returning 1600-1700, costing from around US$45, lunch included; free if staying at one of the hotels. Overnight trips can be arranged through agencies, but they are overpriced. Note that there is an additional 'port tax' of US$6 payable at the entrance to the Muelle or on the boat. Book in advance. For five or more, try hiring your own boat for the day and bargain your price. This way you get to see what you want in the time available. The tour boats leave you with plenty of time with the beach vendors. For the cheapest rates, buy tickets from the boat owners (make sure they are the boat owners!) at the dockside, but they may already be booked up. **Aventure Colombia** (see above) organizes sailboat tours of the islands.

If you wish to enjoy the islands at your leisure there are several hotels to stay in. Recommended is **Isla del Pirata**, which has a number of simple, comfortable *cabañas* and where fresh fish and lobster are served for lunch and dinner. On neighbouring Isla Grande is **San Pedro de Majagua**, owned by Hotel Santa Clara in Cartagena. Snorkelling and diving organizers **Cultura del Mar** also have an ecohotel here, where you can sleep in hammocks or beds, with cooking provided by a local family. ▸▸ *For further information, see Where to stay, page 46.*

South of Cartagena → For listings, see pages 46-51.

Just a few years ago, the area south of Cartagena was a no-go zone. The road between Cartagena and Medellín was the scene of frequent kidnappings by guerrillas who would perform raids on passing traffic and quickly abscond into the region's network of densely vegetated hills. Today it's a different story, and locals no longer sweat before making what was once a perilous journey. However, a word of warning: this area is still very much active in drug trafficking. Towns such as Sincelejo and Montería are fine to pass through but we advise against staying there too long. It is now considered reasonably safe to travel at night between Cartagena and Medellín.

The improvement in security also means that this area, rich in culture and natural wonders, has opened up to tourism. Southwest of Cartagena, on an island in the middle of the imperious Magadalena, is the equally regal town of Mompós (also spelt Mompox). Due south is Tolú, gateway to the coral islands of San Bernardo (also part of the Corales de Rosario and San Bernardo National Park), while further along the coast is Arboletes, location of the largest mud volcano in the area. Further still is Turbo, a rough frontier town from where boats can be caught to the emerald green coastline of the Darién.

Mompós → *Phone code: 5. Population 41,585.*

Arriving in Mompós To reach Mompós from Cartagena there are three options: a direct bus leaves at 0700, US$17 (negotiable). Alternatively, take a bus to Magangue, a *chalupa* (motorized canoe), US$3.50, followed by *colectivo* from La Bodega, US$4 per person. Lastly, a *colectivo* direct from your hotel will cost US$33, call T312-622 5946 (mob). The **Secretaría de Turismo Municipio de Mompós** ① *Calle Real del Medio, Palacio de San Carlos, T685 5919, Mon-Fri 0700-1200 and 1400-1700.* ➻ *For further information, see Transport, page 50.*

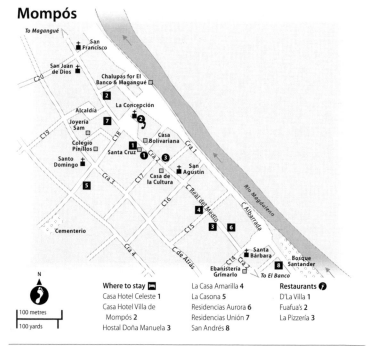

Mompós

Where to stay 🛏
Casa Hotel Celeste **1**
Casa Hotel Villa de
  Mompós **2**
Hostal Doña Manuela **3**
La Casa Amarilla **4**
La Casona **5**
Residencias Aurora **6**
Residencias Unión **7**
San Andrés **8**

Restaurants 🍴
D'La Villa **1**
Fuafua's **2**
La Pizzería **3**

Places south of Cartagena Thanks to a geographical anomaly, Mompós (officially known as Santa Cruz de Mompós) retains much the same atmosphere you might have experienced visiting this sleepy town in the early 20th century. The grand old Magdalena River splits in two just before Mompós. When the town was founded in 1537, the Mompós branch of the river was the main tributary and it became a major staging port for travellers and merchandise going to the interior. But at the beginning of the 20th century it silted up with mud and became unnavigable for large boats, so traffic was diverted to the Brazo de Lobo. As a result, Mompós became a backwater and it has remained practically untouched ever since.

In 1995 UNESCO declared it a World Heritage Site for the quality of its colonial architecture and its fine churches, and it was the setting for the film adaptation of Gabriel García Márquez's *Chronicle of a Death Foretold (1987)*.

Today, in the evenings, as the soporific heat begins to lessen and the bats start to swoop from the eaves of the whitewashed houses, locals carry their rocking chairs out onto the streets to chat with neighbours and watch the world go by. Cars are rare here, the main forms of transport are bicycle, moped, auto-rickshaw – or on foot.

Mompós is still a difficult place to reach – while direct buses are possible, most journeys include a combination of bus, motorized canoe and car. But plans are afoot to improve transport connections. Hopefully, these changes won't detract from its languid charm.

The churches demonstrate the colonial origins of the town; five of the six are close to the centre. The church of **San Francisco** is probably the oldest, dating from the end of the 16th century, with an interesting interior. **Santa Bárbara**, on Calle 14 by the river, has a unique octagonal Moorish tower and balcony. **San Juan de Dios, La Concepción, Santo Domingo** and **San Agustín** are all worth visiting. You may have to ask around for the key to see inside, they are not normally open except during Mass. Among the old buildings are the Casa de Gobierno, once a home of the Jesuits and now the **Alcaldía**, and the **Colegio Pinillos**. The cemetery is of considerable historical interest. Try to visit it on the Wednesday of Semana Santa when it is illuminated by thousands of candles lit by the locals to honour the dead. The town is well known in Colombia for hand-worked gold and silver jewellery, especially filigree, as well as its wicker rocking chairs.

Mompós was particularly dear to Simón Bolívar, as it was the site of one of the greatest victories in his campaign to expel the Spanish from South America. "If to Caracas I owe my life, then to Mompós I owe my glory," he said. He stayed in what is now called the **Casa Bolivariana**, which houses memorabilia of his times and also has some religious art exhibits. The **Casa de la Cultura** is a particularly interesting colonial building and home of the local Academy of History.

Ferocious mosquitoes and the odd bat are a nuisance after dusk; take insect repellent and wear long sleeves.

Tolú → *Phone code: 5.*

Tolú, 35 km northwest of Sincelejo, on the coast, is a fast developing holiday town popular with Colombians and, increasingly, foreign tourists attracted by visits to the offshore islands and diving. Along the *malecón* (promenade), there are plenty of bars and restaurants. A distinctive feature of the town are the bicycle rickshaws armed with loud soundsystems blasting out vallenato, salsa and reggaeton. The rickshaw drivers spend much of their time trying to outdo each other with the volume of their music. Tolú can also be reached more directly from Cartagena, through **San Onofre**, then, after 46 km from San Onofre, turn right for Tolú. Continue straight on from Toluviejo for 20 km to Sincelejo.

A good boat trip from Tolú is to the beautiful beaches of Múcura island or Titipán (**$** *cabañas*) in the **Islas de San Bernardo**, about US$25, 45 minutes. Trips to the mangrove lagoons are also recommended. **Club Náutico Mundo Marino**, run daily boats to San Bernardo Islands at 0830, returning at 1230, which cost US$25 return trip. Isla Múcura has a number of shacks serving seafood, including excellent barbecued lobster. The beach is of fine white sand with beautiful, clear water. Unfortunately, with several launches converging on the island at the same time, it can get crowded and the number of beach vendors can detract from the beauty of the place. There is a charge for everything, including sitting at a table. To enjoy the islands at your leisure, it is better to stay overnight. It's also possible to reach the island from Cartagena, if you have a reservation at Punta Faro (one hour 45 minutes by boat, transfer included in the cost of accommodation. ›› *For further information, see Where to stay and What to do, pages 46 and 50.*

There are, perhaps surprisingly, good beaches at **Coveñas**, 20 km further southwest, the terminal of the oil pipeline from the oilfields in the Venezuelan border area. Coveñas is essentially a 5-km-long stretch of road peppered with *cabañas* and hotels. During high season (Easter, Christmas-mid January, June and July) it is very popular with Colombians eager to hit the beach and party. To get there, take a bus or *colectivo* from Tolú.

Further along the coast, turning right 18 km southwest of Coveñas at Lorica is **San Bernardo del Viento** from where launches can be arranged to **Isla Fuerte**, an unspoilt coral island with fine beaches and simple places to stay. It's a good place to dive, but there are very limited facilities on the island. Enquire at travel agencies in Medellín and elsewhere for inclusive trips or negotiate in San Bernardo.

Arboletes

Southwest of Tolú is the unremarkable town of Arboletes which nonetheless has an extraordinary attraction: the largest mud volcano in the area. Dipping into this swimming pool-sized mud bath is a surreal experience – like swimming in treacle. It's also very good for your skin. You can wash the mud off in the sea by walking to the beach 100 m below. Arboletes is also a convenient stopover on the way to Turbo and the Darién coast.

The **Volcán de Lodo** is a 15-minute walk from town on the road to Montería or a two-minute taxi ride (US$5.50 return – the driver will wait for you while you bathe). A mototaxi costs US$1. There is a small restaurant and changing rooms (US$ 0.30), plus a locker room (US$1 per bag) and showers (US$0.50).

Turbo

At the mouth of the Gulf of Urabá is the port of Turbo, a hot, rough, frontier community with a lawless feel about it. It is a centre for banana cultivation. There is little reason to stop here except to catch a boat to Capurganá and the Panamanian border.

The Darién Gap

The Darién Gap has long held a special place in travellers' lore as the ultimate adventure – and with reason. This thin stretch of land, just 50 km wide and 160 km long, which links Central and South America, has some of the densest tropical jungle in the world – so dense that to date neither the Panamanians nor the Colombians have succeeded in building a road across. There are no roads of any kind, the only inland routes are by boat or on foot. At present, the Pan-American Highway from Canada to Tierra del Fuego in Chile stops at Yaviza in Panama, 60 km short of the frontier, and begins again 27 km west of Barranquillita, well into Colombia. The Darién is home to an incredible profusion of flora and fauna, as well as indigenous tribes who rarely see foreigners.

The trek across the Darién is held in high regard by adventurers but we strongly advise against it, not simply because it is easy and fatal to get lost, but also because bona fide travellers are not welcome (indigenous communities still living in Darién have never truly accepted trekkers passing through) and this area still has a heavy guerrilla presence. The Colombian government's successes against the FARC have pushed them to the extremes of the country, where they have retreated to lick their wounds. Those trafficking drugs from South to North America have found the density of the jungle a useful protection for running consignments. Both FARC and ELN guerrilla groups have infiltrated the region and paramilitaries regard this as a threat to their land. As a result this has become a violent war zone, virtually deserted now by police and the military, and it is a hostile environment for any tourist. As recently as 2008 there were reports of kidnappings in the Darién. For the moment only the foolhardy will attempt the land crossing. However, the Caribbean coastline, heavily patrolled by Colombian and Panamanian forces, is safe, though you should exercise caution if venturing into the forest beyond.

Acandí
Acandí is a small fishing village on the Caribbean side of the Darién. It has a spectacular, forest-fringed bay with turquoise waters. In April, thousands of leatherback turtles come here to lay their eggs. There are several cheap *residencias* to stay in. There are several flights a week from Medellín with **Aerolínea de Antioquia** (www.ada-aero.com) (US$120 one way).

Capurganá
For many years, Capurganá and neighbouring Sapzurro have been one of the best kept secrets in Colombia. In this most isolated of Colombia's corners, a glistening, untouched shoreline of crystal waters and coral reefs backs onto quiet little villages where, at night, if you listen carefully, you can hear the howler monkeys calling to each other in the jungle-clad hills behind.

Capurganá has developed into a resort popular with affluent Colombians and is increasingly visited by foreigners, despite it being somewhat difficult or expensive to get to. Until fairly recently it was an important point for smuggling drugs through to Panama, with heavy guerrilla activity. But a strong army presence has put an end to that and it is now considered a safe place to visit. It is a quiet place: there are no cars and just two motorbikes. Taxi rides are provided by horse and carts, and someone has had the ingenious idea of attaching modified plastic seats.

There are two beaches in the village. La Caleta is at the northern end, beyond the pontoon, and is protected by a barrier reef, has golden sand and is the best for swimming. There are a couple of restaurants and several hotels and *cabañas* here. Playa de los Pescadores, south of the village, is fringed by palm and almond trees but has disappointing grey sand and is more pebbly. Ask the fishermen about fishing trips from here (US$ 15-20 in rowing boats).

Around Capurganá

Several half- and full-day trips can be made by launch boat to neighbouring beaches. Aguacate is a beautiful bay with clear, aquamarine water and a small beach. There is a rocky promontory with a blowhole and what locals call '*La Piscina*', a natural jacuzzi amongst the rocks which you can lower yourself into using a rope. There is also a small restaurant serving fried fish for US$7. Aguacate has good snorkelling, but Playa Soledad is perhaps the most attractive beach in the area and was recently used as the location for a Colombian reality TV programme. The beach is white sand and fringed by palms.

A return trip by launch boat costs US$11 per person, minimum five people. You can also walk to Aguacate, 1½ hours along the coast, though not to Playa Soledad. Note that it can be difficult to obtain a return by launch if you walk.

Another trip is to Sapzurro, a few kilometres north (see below). **Capurganá Tours** organizes day trips to the San Blas archipelago in Panama, possibly some of the most beautiful islands in the Caribbean and launches stop at the island of Caledonia (US$55-60 per person with a minimum of 28 people).

There is excellent diving and snorkelling around Capurganá. You are likely to see nurse sharks, moray eels, spotted eagle rays, trumpetfish, jewfish, barracuda and hawksbill turtles, among other species, as well as large brain and elkhorn coral. Several of the hotels organize diving and the independent dive centre, **Dive and Green**, near the jetty is recommended.

A delightful half-day excursion is to **El Cielo** ① *entry US$2*, a small waterfall in the jungle. You can walk there in 40 minutes through beautiful primary jungle. Take flip flops or waterproof boots, as you will have to cross a stream several times and it is muddy. Take the path to the left of the airport and keep asking for directions as it is easy to get lost. Just before the waterfall there is a small restaurant serving *patacones* and drinks. There is a swimming hole with a zip wire. Alternatively, you can hire horses to take you there (US$7).

Another horse-riding trip is to El Valle de Los Ríos, a valley in the jungle with several crystalline rivers and beautiful waterfalls. The primary forest in this area is rich in wildlife; you might see, among other animals, sloths, howler monkeys, toucans, parrots, fishing eagles and several types of lizard and iguana. You should take a guide for this. The trip includes lunch at a *ranchería*. For more details, enquire at **Capurganá Tours** in town, by the jetty, or at the football pitch (*cancha de futbol*) in the village centre.

Sapzurro

Sapzurro is a quiet little village in the Darién and the last outpost before Panama and Central America. Set in a shallow, horseshoe-shaped bay dotted with coral reefs, little happens in this village of less than 1000 inhabitants. There are no roads, let alone cars; the houses are linked by intersecting pathways bursting with tropical flowers. It has a couple of excellent little hostels and some good restaurants serving up home-cooked seafood. The bay is excellent for snorkelling, with a couple of underwater caves to explore.

You can make a day trip to the small village of **La Miel** over the border in Panama by walking up the forested hill behind the village. This could qualify as the most relaxed border crossing in the world. The Colombian and Panamanian immigration offiers share a hut and copy each other's notes. Be sure to take your passport; if only going to La Miel they won't stamp it but they will take your details. There are breathtaking views of Panama and back into Sapzurro at the border crossing on the brow of the hill.

La Miel has a gorgeous white-sand beach with beautiful, clear waters and a coral reef. The snorkelling is relatively good though a little low on fauna. There are a couple of shacks selling beer and food. Try the sea snails in coconut sauce. You can arrange for a launch to pick you up and take you back to Sapzurro or Capurganá.

◉ Around Cartagena listings → *Phone code: 5.*

For sleeping and eating price codes and other relevant information, see pages 8-13.

◯ Where to stay

Islas del Rosario *p39*

$$$ Isla del Pirata, book through **Hotel Isla Pirata**, C 6 No 2-26, Bocagrande, T665 2952, www.hotelislapirata.com. 12 comfortable *cabañas* with activities that include diving, snorkelling, canoeing and petanque. Fresh fish and lobster are served for lunch and dinner. Prices include transport to the island, food and non-guided activities. Highly recommended.

Isla Grande
$$$ San Pedro de Majagua, book at Calle del Torno, No 39-29, T650 4460, www.hotel majagua.com. Everything from a 'pillow menu' to Egyptian cotton bed sheets, this is a lovely, luxurious place for utter relaxation.

Mompós *p41, map p41*
Almost all of the hotels in Mompós are located on C Real del Medio, the main thoroughfare through town which boasts beautifully preserved whitewashed houses with enormous iron grills. Note that most hotels in Mompós double in price over Semana Santa and other festival periods.
$$$ Hostal Doña Manuela, C Real del Medio (Cra 2), 17-41, T685 5621/5142, hostal mompox@turiscolombia.com. A charming hotel converted from the largest colonial house in town, centred around a courtyard with an extraordinary banyan tree. The rooms are spacious and fresh, while its swimming pool at the back provides welcome respite from the soporific heat. With an art gallery

and jewellery shop and its central position, it is often at the hub of the action. Accepts credit cards.
$$ Casa Hotel Celeste, C Real del Medio (Cra 2), No 14-174, T685 6875. Decorated with old photographs and fake oil paintings, this hotel is just the right side of chintzy. Rooms are a little small.
$$ Casa Hotel Villa de Mompós, 500 m east of Parque Bolívar, Cra 2 No 14-108, T685 5208. Charming family-run hotel, decorated with antique bric-a-brac. Internet access US$1 per hr. Can also arrange rooms for families during festival periods.
$$ Hacienda San Ignacio, a few kilometres out of town on the road to Talaigua. This modern hacienda, built on land belonging to Jesuit priests may offer welcome respite from the sometimes oppressive heat of Mompós. Rooms are clean and simple, it has a swimming pool and offers horse riding. It is managed by **Hostal Doña Manuela** (see above); ask there for details.
$$ La Casona, Cra 2, No 18-58, T685 5307, eusedeal@yahoo.es. Fine colonial building with delightful courtyards and plants. Has a billiard table, TV, a/c, laundry service and internet access. Just pips the rest of them for atmosphere.
$$ Residencias Aurora, Cra 2, No 15-65, T685 5723. Dishevelled but with character. Some shared baths, big ceilings, kitchen available, security could be an issue.
$$ San Andrés, Cra 2, No 18-23, T855 886. Another fine, restored colonial building. The patio has parrots and aquariums. Rooms have TV and bathroom. Has own water and electricity supply (useful during power cuts). Can arrange guides for local area.

$$-$ La Casa Amarilla, C 13 No 1-05, T685 6326, www.lacasaamarillamompos.com. 1 block up from Iglesia Santa Bárbara on the riverfront, this backpackers' hostel has 6 luxury rooms with a/c, bath and cable TV, 3 economic rooms with bath and fan, and an a/c dorm (**$** pp), beautifully decorated. The hostel boasts 2 living rooms equipped with TV and DVD player, a book exchange and an information board while at the end of the garden there is an open-plan kitchen for guests' use. English owner and travel journalist Richard McColl is an excellent source of information on Colombia.

$ Residencias Unión, C 18, No 3-43, T685 5723. The only hotel in Mompós in a modern building. The rooms are cheap but a little dark and likely to be noisy during festivities as hotel is near the action. No double beds available.

Tolú p42

$$ Alcira, Av La Playa, No 21-151, T288 5016, alcirahotel@yahoo.com. On the promenade, has a breezy courtyard and lots of balconies with rocking chairs. Has a/c, laundry service, parking, restaurant and Wi-Fi. Breakfast included.

$$ Playamar, Av La Playa, No 22-22, T286 0587, playamar@yahoo.es. Large, white building on the *malecón* with beautiful lemon trees outside. Has all the mod cons, including Wi-Fi, a/c, minibar, parking and TV. Has a small restaurant serving breakfast.

$$-$ pp Estado Natural Ecolodge, 7 km from San Bernardo del Viento, T301-442 2438, www.estado-natural.com. Rustic cabins with kitchen on beach; meals not included. Composting toilets and other sustainable practices. Birdwatching, windsurfing, trips to Isla Fuerte, riding and guided tours available.

$ Altamar, Cra 3, No 17-36, T288 5421. Bright rooms opening onto an open-air corridor. Has its own water and electricity supply. Prices more than double in high season.

$ Darimar, C 17, No 1-60, T288 5153. Just off the beach front with small but clean rooms, private bathrooms, TV and parking. Friendly staff.

$ El Turista, Av La Playa, No 11-20, T288 5145. The cheapest option in town and good value for money. On the promenade, next to all the tour agencies.

$ Los Angeles, C 17, No 1-23, T300-600 6107. Right on beach with TV, fan and private bathrooms, though the rooms are crammed with as many beds as possible.

$ Mar Adentro, Av La Playa, No 11-36, T286 0079. Hotel belonging to tour agency of same name. Nice, clean rooms with private bathrooms. Rooms are cheaper with fan.

$ Villa Babilla, C 20, No 3-40, Barrio el Cangrejo, T288 6124, www.villababilla hostel.com. Easily the best option in Tolú. Colombian/German couple Alex and Laffie have built a quiet little haven of simple, brightly painted rooms with a thatched *cabaña* as a TV area and lots of hammocks. Alex is a good source of information on activities in local area.

Isla Múcura

$$$$ Punta Faro, Isla Múcura, Islas San Bernardo, T318-323 2323, www.punta faro.com. Low-key luxury resort with 45 rooms in gorgeous setting by the sea, inside Corales del Rosario y San Bernardo National Park. Price includes all meals, buffet-style, and return boat transfer from Cartagena (boats leave once a day in high season and Mon and Fri only in low season, so make sure you catch it). Massage treatments, hammocks on the beach, eco walks around the island and a good sustainability policy. Highly recommended.

Coveñas

$$$ Villa Melissa, T288 0249, www.hotel villamelissa.com. Large apartments on the beach each with their own balcony, a/c and TV. Also has a swimming pool.

$ Cabañas del Morrosquillo, Km 9 Vía Tolú, T280 0341. Not the prettiest concrete structures you have ever seen but have comfortable beds and fan. On a good, quiet stretch of beach.

Arboletes *p43*

$ Ganadero, C Principal, T820 0086. Basic but clean rooms. Has a pleasant reception area under a thatched hut and a restaurant serving basic fare for US$3.50.

$ La Floresta, C Principal, T820 0034. Opposite **Ganadero**, this small hotel has simple rooms with private bathrooms. Ask for a street-facing room if you want a window.

Turbo *p43*

$$ Castilla de Oro, C 100, No 14-07, T827 2185. The best option in town, has a/c, safety box, minibar, a good restaurant and a swimming pool. Modern building with reliable water and electricity. Friendly staff.

$$ Hotel 2000, C 101, No 12-115, T827 2333. Next to bus terminal, rooms with TV and private bathrooms. Almost half the price if you choose a room with fan only.

$$ Simona del Mar, Km 13 Vía Turbo, T824 3729, www.simonadelmar.com. Turbo is not a safe place in which to walk around at night, so this is a better, safer option for sleeping. A few kilometres outside town, this hotel has a number of *cabañas* in a tranquil setting and near the beach. Has good restaurant. The beach is nice enough, although like everywhere on this stretch of the coast, the sea is a muddy brown due to its proximity to the Gulf of Urabá. A taxi to and from Turbo is US$11. You can also ask *colectivos* to drop you there.

$$-$ Playa Mar, Av de la Playa, T827 2205. Good, but somewhat run down with a restaurant. Has a/c, TV and is cheaper with fan.

Acandí *p44*

$$ pp Al Vaivén de Hamacas, San Francisco, T321-643 1171, http://alvaiven reserva.blog spot.com. Price is half board, cheaper without bath, Colombian food, a resort accessible by boat from Turbo (leaves between 0830 and 0900, between 1200 and 1230) or Capurganá (0730, 1 hr), with trekking and horse riding on the beach or in the jungle, boat tours, kayak tours to nearby islands, fishing and river bathing, English spoken.

Capurganá *p44*

Accomodation is generally more expensive than in other parts of Colombia but it is possible to find reasonably cheap hostels.

$$$$ Almar, enquire through offices in Medellín, T436 6262, www.almar.com.co. Luxury wooden *cabañas* amongst manicured gardens and right on the beach. Has Turkish bath, spa, jacuzzi and a pool.

$$$ Playa de Capurganá, T276 4260 (Medellín) T094-824 3914 (Capurganá), www.jardinbotanicodarien.com/condo minio.htm. Set in tropical gardens, this breezy wooden house has comfortable rooms with private bathrooms and a fine veranda with hammocks from which to look out to sea, as well as a great swimming pool right on the beach. The price includes a home-cooked breakfast and dinner. Recommended.

$$$ Tacarcuna Lodge, T361 7809 (Medellín), www.hotelesdecostaacosta.com. *Cabañas* around a garden pool. All meals included.

$$ Cabaña Darius, T314-622 5638, www.dariuscapurgana.es.tl. In the grounds of Playa de Capurganá, this is excellent value for money with simple, comfortable rooms in a wooden chalet set in exquisite tropical gardens. Large balconies with hammocks. Rooms have fan, private bathroom and breakfast is included.

$$ Hostal Marlin, Playa de los Pescadores, T824 3611, capurganamarlin@yahoo.es. The best mid-range option in town. A beautiful wooden chalet with good rooms, private bathrooms and a patio with a mango tree and lots of plants and songbirds. Has a good restaurant serving excellent fish. There are also bunks (**$**) available.

$ Hostal Capurganá, C del Comercio, T316-743 3863. Comfortable, clean rooms with private bathrooms. Has a pleasant patio and is well situated on the main street, next to the jetty. Recommended.

$ Los Delfines, T682 8788. A few blocks back from the jetty, rooms are very basic but there are pretty balconies with hammocks, a restaurant and TV.

$ Luz de Oriente, T824 3719, luzdeoriente 999@hotmail.com. Right on the jetty, each of the rooms is named after a *Lord of the Rings* character. Rooms are a bit cramped with too many beds. Has a beautiful restaurant serving average food.

Private houses

Cabaña de los Alemanes, a simple self-catering bungalow with a thatched hut for slinging hammocks and a small plunge pool. The *cabaña* is in a prime position, right on the waterfront – the sea laps against the edge of the garden. Sleeps 8 in bunks and single beds for US$150 per night. Enquire at **Dive and Green**, page 50, for more details.

Sapzurro p45

$$ Hostería Zingara, Camino La Miel, T313-673 3291. Pretty much the last building before you get to Panama, **Zingara** has 2 lovely *cabañas* with gorgeous views over the bay. The owners have a herb and vegetable garden and sell home-made chutneys. This also doubles up as the village pharmacy.

$ Paraíso Sapzurro, T824 4115/T313-685 9862, www.paraiso-sapzurro-colombia.com. Right on the beach at the southern end of the village, this has a number of *cabañas*, a little more basic than **Zingara**'s, run by a charismatic Chilean. Has an excellent thatched ranch full of hammocks for relaxing. Also has space for camping. Ask for El Chileno and you will be directed here when you arrive. Higher price includes half-board.

Restaurants

Mompós p41, map p41
Good bakeries on C 18 and Cra 3 for coffee, cakes and snacks. A selection of fast-food kiosks can be found at the Plaza Santo Domingo, next to the church.

$$$ Restaurante Doña Manuela, part of the hostel of the same name (see Where to stay), probably the best restaurant in town (though pricey with it), fish is particularly good, try the *bagre momposino*.

$$ Fuafua's, on Parque Bolívar, T684 0609. Serves *comida corriente*, worth going to if just to experience its grand old dilapidated dining hall looking out over the square.

$$ La Pizzería, opposite San Agustín Church. Good pizzas in a lovely setting.

$ D'La Villa, C 18, No 2-49, T685 8793. For those tired of chicken and steak this bakery/ice cream parlour also serves up a selection of crêpes.

$ La Parcela, a few kilometers out of town opposite the airport, open only on Sun. Momposinos go here to sit under the shade of mango trees and eat *sancocho* and *ajiaco* while listening to *vallenato*.

Tolú p42

$ La 15, Av La Playa, No 15 esquina. Good steaks and swift service. Recommended.

$ La Atarraya, C 15, No 1-38. Cheap fast food. Burgers, pizza and hotdogs.

$ La Red, Av La Playa, No 20. Decorated with all things aquatic, including fishing nets, star fish, turtle shells, oars and model boats. Serves cheap but good seafood, steaks, burgers and hotdogs. Friendly staff.

$ Punto B, C 15, No 2-02. Cheap and cheerful restaurant and *panadería* serving the usual Colombian fare. *menú del día*, US$ 3.

Capurganá p44

$$ Donde Josefina, Playa La Caleta, T316-779 7760. Josefina cooks exquisite seafood, served to you under a shady tree on the beach. Try the lobster cooked in garlic and coconut sauce.

$ El Patacón, C del Comercio. Serves good, simple seafood.

$ Luz de Oriente, on the jetty. Lovely looking restaurant decorated with lots of hanging shells, though the food is a bit bland.

$ Pizzería Mi Ciclo, T314-789 1826. This isn't a restaurant as much as a lovely woman who will cook remarkably good pizzas from an oven in her bedsit and bring out a table and chairs for you to eat them on. Ask around for her on the C del Comercio, near Capurganá Tours.

Sapzurro *p45*
$ La Negra, C Principal. Serves home-cooked seafood.

🎭 Entertainment

Mompós *p41, map p41*
There are a number of bars and discos along the riverfront, among the best of which is the bohemian **Luna de Mompox**.

🛍 Shopping

Mompós *p41, map p41*
Mompós is famous for its filigree gold and silver jewellery and its wicker rocking chairs. You can visit workshops.

Jewellery
Joyería Sam, C 18A No 2B, T685 5829. Fine selection of beautifully worked gold and silver earrings, bracelets and brooches.
Santa Cruz, Cra 2, No 20-132, T685 6371, tallersantacruz@yahoo.com.

Rocking chairs
Ebanistería Grimarlo, Cra 2, No 13-29, T685 5313.
Muebles Momposinos, Cra 2, opposite Monumento del Sagrado Corazón, T685 5349.

⛰ What to do

Islas del Rosario *p39*

Diving
Cultura del Mar, Getsemaní C del Pozo, No 25-95, Cartagena, T664 9312. Offices in Cartagena, organizes snorkelling and diving,

and various tours of the coral reefs and mangroves of the islands.
Excursiones Roberto Lemaitre, C 6 No 2-26, Edificio Granada, local 2, Bocagrande, T665 5622 (owner of **Club Isla del Pirata**). They have the best boats and are near the top end of the price range but **Yates Alcatraz** is more economical; enquire at the quay.

Tolú *p42*

Tour operators
Club Náutico Mar Adentro, Av La Playa, No 11-36, T286 0079, www.clubnauticomar adentro.com. A good agency.

Capurganá *p44*

Diving
Dive and Green, near the jetty, T682 8825, www.diveandgreen.com. The only dive centre in town that does PADI. Has a 27 ft boat with 200 horsepower. Excursions to San Blas. English spoken.

Tour operators
Capurganá Tours, C del Comercio, T316 4823665, www.capurganatours.net. Organizes walking tours with knowledgeable guides to nearby beaches and into the jungle as well as horse riding, diving and birdwatching. Trips to San Blas islands in Panama arranged if sufficient people. Can assist in booking flights from Puerto Obaldía to Panama City. English spoken. Highly recommended.

🚌 Transport

Mompós *p41, map p41*

Bus
To **Cartagena** there are 3 options: with **Unitransco**, direct, US$17 (negotiable), bus leaves at 0600 from outside Iglesia Santa Barbara; or *colectivo* to La Bodega, US$4 per person, *chalupa* (motorized canoe) US$3.50, and finally bus to Magangué. **Asotranstax**

runs a door-to-door *colectivo* service between Mompós and Santa Marta, US$30; and Mompós and Valledupar. To **Medellín**, taxi to La Bodega, then *chalupa* to Magangué and finally bus with **Brasilia** or **Rápido Ochoa**, 10 hrs, US$45. Alternatively, take a bus to Santa Ana via Aracataca and Bosconia, then a *chalupa* to Talaigua, and finally a *colectivo*.

Unitransco has direct service to **Barranquilla**, leaving at 0600. To **Bogotá**, **Copetran** and **Omega** have services leaving from El Banco (4WD trip from Mompós) at 1600, US$27-39. To **Bucaramanga**, a **Copetran** bus leaves El Banco at 1000. Return journey leaves Bucaramanga at 1000.

Tolú *p42*

Bus
Brasilia has buses every hour to **Cartagena** between 0715 and 1730. 12 a day to **Medellín** with Brasilia and Rápido Ochoa, US$40, via Montería except at night. **Bogotá**, 3 a day, US$55. To **Barranquilla**, **Santa Marta** and **Riohacha**, 5 a day, US$33. For **Bucaramanga** you must change at Sincelejo, 2 a day, US$55. To **Valledupar**, 1 a day, changing at Sincelejo, US$25.

Turbo *p43*

Sea
Launches for **Acandí**, **Capurganá** and **Sapzurro** leave daily at 0800, US$25 and take 3 hrs. It's a spectacular journey that hugs the Caribbean shoreline of the Darién. As passengers begin to embark you will notice a rush for seats at the back. You are well advised to join in the scrum as the journey is bumpy and can be painful in seats at the front. **Note** There is a 10 kg limit on baggage, excess is US$0.50 per kg. Between mid-Dec and the end of Feb the sea becomes very choppy and dangerous. We advise you not to make this journey during this period.

Capurganá *p44*

Air
1 flight daily to **Medellín** with **Aerolínea de Antioquia** (ADA), US$300-350 return. Twin Otter biplanes with 16 passenger capacity. Be sure to book ahead. Baggage limit of 10 kg. Excess is US$2 per kg. You may be asked to allow your baggage to follow on a later plane if seriously overweight.

Sea
There's a launch to **Turbo**, daily, leaving at 0800, US$25. Be sure to get a seat at the back as the 3-hr ride is bumpy and can be excruciatingly uncomfortable at the front.

There are daily launches to **Puerto Obaldía** in Panama, US$20 (leaving at about 0700). From here it's possible to catch an **Air Panamá** flight to **Panama City** on Sun, Tue or Thu, cost US$63, www.flyairpanama.com. Essential to book in advance. It is possible to catch a further launch from Puerto Obaldía to **Mulatupo**, US$20, and from there to **Colón**, US$66.

Sapzurro *p45*
You can walk to **Capurganá** in 4 hrs, a beautiful hike along the coastline through jungle rich in wildlife.

Sea
Launches to **Capurganá** cost US$3, 30 mins. Launches leave from Puerto Obaldía or La Miel to **Panama**. Launch to Puerto Obaldía 45 mins, US$15.

❶ Directory

Capurganá *p44*
Immigration **DAS office**, on the waterfront next to the police station, between the jetty and Playa de los Pescadores, Mon-Fri 0800-1500, Sat, Sun and holidays 0900-1600, T311-746 6234. If leaving for Panama you must get your passport stamped here. For entry into Panama you'll need proof of US$600 in the bank and a yellow fever certificate.

Barranquilla

Barranquilla, Colombia's fourth city, lies on the western bank of the Río Magdalena, about 18 km from its mouth. It's a seaport (though less busy than Cartagena or Santa Marta), as well as a river port, and a modern industrial city with a polluted but colourful central area near the river. First and foremost, however, Barranquilla is famed for its Carnival, reputed to be second only to Rio de Janeiro in terms of size and far less commercialized. In 2003 UNESCO declared it a "masterpiece of the oral and intangible heritage of humanity". Pre-carnival parades and dances last through January until an edict that everyone must party is read out. Carnival itself lasts from Saturday, with the Batalla de las Flores, through the Gran Parada on Sunday, to the funeral of Joselito Carnaval on Tuesday. The same families have been participating for generations, keeping the traditions of the costumes and dances intact. Prepare for three days of intense revelry and dancing with very friendly and enthusiastic crowds, spectacular floats, processions, parades and beauty queens. The main action takes place along Calle 17, Carrera 44 and Vía 40.

Arriving in Barranquilla

Getting there and around Ernesto Cortissoz airport is 10 km from the city. A city bus from the airport to town costs US$0.35 (US$0.40 on Sunday). Only take buses marked 'centro', you can catch them 200 m from the airport on the right. A taxi to town costs US$7 (taxis do not have meters, so agree on the fare in advance). The main **bus terminal** is south of the city near the Circunvalación. Some bus companies have offices around Calle

☐ **Barranquilla centre**

➡ **Barranquilla maps**
1 Barranquilla centre, page 52
2 Barranquilla – El Prado, page 53

Where to stay 🛏
Girasol **3**
Horizonte **4**
Hotel del Mar **2**
San Francisco **5**

Restaurants 🍴
Pescadero El Centro **1**

34 and Carrera 45. If arriving into Barranquilla by boat and shipping your car, allow two days to complete all the paperwork you'll need to retrieve your car from the port. Taxis for trips within town cost US\$1.60. ▸▸ *For more information, see Transport, page 56.*

Tourist information Tourist information is available at the main hotels, at the **tourist office** ① *C40 No 36-135, Edif La Aduana, T351 0415*, and from the **tourist police** ① *Cra 43, No 47-53, T340 9903*.

Places in Barranquilla → *Phone code: 5. Population: 1,148,000.*
The city is surrounded by a continuous ring road called the 'Vía Cuarenta' from the north along the river to the centre; 'Avenida Boyacá' to the bridge (Puente Pumarejo), which crosses the Río Magdalena for Santa Marta; and 'Circunvalación' round the south and west of the city. The long bridge over the Río Magdalena gives fine views.

In the centre the principal boulevard is **Paseo Bolívar** leading to **Parque Simón Bolívar**. Two blocks south is a handsome church, **San Nicolás**, formerly the cathedral, in Plaza San Nicolás, the central square, and before it stands a small statue of Columbus. The more recent **Catedral Metropolitana** ① *Cra 45, No 53-120*, is opposite Parque la Paz. There is an impressive statue of Christ inside by the Colombian sculptor, Arenas Betancourt. Further along is the small **Museo Antropológico** ① *C 68, No 53-45*, which has

2 Barranquilla – El Prado

➡ **Barranquilla maps**
1 Barranquilla centre, page 52
2 Barranquilla – El Prado, page 53

Where to stay 🛏
Barranquilla Plaza 1
Bulevard 58 3
El Prado 2
Majestic 4

Restaurants 🍴
Don Pepe 1
Jardines de Confucio 2
La Fonda Antioqueña 3
La Pizza Loca 4

Los Helechos 5

Bars & clubs 🍸
Froggs Leggs 6
Henry's 7

a big physical relief map on the front lawn, and the **Museo Romántico** ⓘ *Cra 54, No 59-199*, which covers the history of Barranquilla, including the establishment of air services and radio in Colombia, with an interesting section on the local Carnival and a replica of 'Camellón Abello', an old street of Barranquilla.

The commercial and shopping districts are round the Paseo Bolívar, a few blocks north of the old cathedral, and in Avenida Murillo. The colourful and vivid **market** is between Paseo Bolívar and the river, the so-called Zona Negra on a branch of the Río Magdalena. Nearby **Barranquilla Zoo** ⓘ *Calle 77/Carrera 68*, is one of the biggest and best maintained zoos in the country, however many of the animals (some rarely seen in captivity) are kept in small cages. To get there, take bus 'Boston/Boston' or 'Caldes/Recreo'. There are good parks to the northwest of the centre, including **Parque Tomás Suri Salcedo** on Calle 72. Stretching back into the northwestern heights overlooking the city are the modern suburbs of **El Prado**, Altos del Prado, Golf and Ciudad Jardín, where you'll find the El Prado Hotel.

There is a full range of services including commercial and shopping centres, and banks between Bulevar Norte and Avenida Olaya Herrera towards the Country Club. There are five stadiums in the city, a big covered coliseum for sports, two for football, and the others cater for basketball and baseball. The metropolitan stadium is on Avenida Murillo, outside the city where it meets the south stretch of the Circunvalación.

Around Barranquilla

Regular buses from Paseo Bolívar and the church at Calle 33/Carrera 41 go to the attractive bathing resort of **Puerto Colombia**, 19 km, with its pier built around 1900. This was formerly the ocean port of Barranquilla, connected by a railway. The beach is clean and sandy, though the water is a bit muddy. Nearby are the beaches of **Salgar**, and north of Barranquilla is **Las Flores** (2 km from the mouth of the Río Magdalena at Bocas de Ceniza), both good places for seafood.

South along the west bank of the Magdalena, 5 km from the city, is the old colonial town of **Soledad**. The cathedral and the old narrow streets around it are worth seeing. A further 25 km south is **Santo Tomás**, known for its Good Friday flagellants who symbolically whip themselves as an Easter penance. There are also street theatre presentations at this time. The small town of **Palmar de Varela** is a little further along the same road, which continues on to Calamar.

⊙ Barranquilla listings → *Phone code: 5.*

⊖ Where to stay

Barranquilla *p52, maps p52 and p53*
Hotel prices tend to double during Carnival. Watch out for thieves in downtown hotels.
$$$$-$$$ El Prado, Cra 54, No 70-10, T369 7777, www.hotelelpradosa.com. A landmark in Barranquilla, this enormous hotel with 200 rooms has been around since 1930 and still retains some of its old-fashioned service. It has a fantastic pool shaded by palm trees, various restaurants, tennis courts and a gym.
$$$ Barranquilla Plaza, Cra 51B, No 79-246, T361 0333, www.hbp.com.co. A deluxe hotel popular with Colombian businessmen, it's worth visiting just for the 360° view of the city from its 26th-floor restaurant. It has all the other amenities you would expect of a hotel of this standard, including gym, spa, sauna and Wi-Fi.

$$$ Hotel Majestic, Cra 53, No 54-41, T349 1010, www.hotelmajesticcolombia.com. An oasis of calm from the bustle of Barranquilla, the **Majestic** has a fine pool and large, fresh rooms as well as a restaurant serving the usual fish and meat dishes and sandwiches.

$$ Hotel Bulevard 58, Cra 58, No 70-41, T368 0810, www.hotelbulevard58.com. It has an 1980s feel about it even though it was apparently only converted from a residential home in the 1990s. Breakfast is included, and it has a pool, and Wi-Fi available in all rooms.

$$ Hotel San Francisco, C 43, No 43-128, T351 5532, www.sfcol.com/barranquilla. With modern, bright, clean rooms and a courtyard full of songbirds, this is a good, safe bet. It also offers laundry, a restaurant and internet services.

$ Hotel del Mar, C 42, No 35-57, T341 3703. Popular with locals, this is probably the best option for those on a budget. The rooms are clean and bright, the service friendly and the food in its restaurant cheap. Good value.

$ Hotel Girasol, C 44, No 44-103, T379 3191, www.elhotelgirasol.com. It's clean, safe and has a restaurant and Wi-Fi in all rooms, but it doesn't offer much in terms of character.

$ Horizonte, Cra 44, No 44-35, T341 7925. Dingy and dark but just about passes.

🍴 Restaurants

Barranquilla *p52, maps p52 and p53*

In Barranquilla you'll find places to suit all tastes and budgets. There are Lebanese restaurants with belly-dancers, Chinese restaurants and pizzerias. The best selection is on C 70 from **Hotel El Prado** towards Cra 42. At C 70 y 44B you'll find several *estaderos*, bars with snacks and verandas.

$$ Jardines de Confucio, Cra 54, No 75-44. Classy Chinese restaurant with a large menu and a good atmosphere.

$ Don Pepe, Cra 53, No 53-90, T349 1062. Opposite the **Hotel Majestic**, it has a breezy patio serving up *comida santandereana*.

$ La Fonda Antioqueña, Cra 52, No 70-73, T360 0573. Just across the road from **Los Helechos** and serving the same fare, but it has a fine patio with draping flowers.

$ La Pizza Loca, Cra 53, No 70-97, also at C 84, No 50-36. Pizzería.

$ Los Helechos, Cra 52, No 70-70, T356 7493. Around the corner from **Hotel El Prado**, this popular restaurant serves up typical *comida antioqueña*, including *sancochos* and *ajiacos*, in a good atmosphere.

$ Pescadero del Centro, Cra 44, No 42-43. A favourite, seving local seafood.

🍸 Bars and clubs

Barranquilla *p52, maps p52 and p53*

Froggs Leggs, C 93, No 43-122. Popular bar, good atmosphere. Open Thu-Sun.

Henry's Bar, C 80, No 53-18, Local 25. Open daily from 1600, until late. Popular US-style bar, with a pizzeria downstairs.

🎭 Entertainment

Barranquilla *p52, maps p52 and p53*
Teatro Amira de la Rosa. This modern theatre offers a full range of stage presentations, concerts, ballets, art exhibitions, etc throughout the year.

🎉 Festivals

Barranquilla *p52, maps p52 and p53*
Jan/Feb Carnival, tickets for the spectator stands are sold in major restaurants and bars, eg **Froggs Leggs** (see Bars and clubs, above). **La Casa de Carnaval**, Carrera 54, No 49B-39, T379 6625, www.carnavaldebarranquilla.org, is the official office and the best place to get information. Carnival is a long-standing tradition in Barranquilla, lasting for the 4 days before Ash Wed, comparable to the carnivals of Rio de Janeiro and Trinidad. There are parades, floats, street dancing, beauty contests and general mayhem. As always on such occasions, take special care of your valuables.

Shopping

Barranquilla *p52, maps p52 and p53*

Bookshop
Librería Nacional, CC Buenavista, Cra 53, No 98-99 esq, local 225. Has a small selection of English books.

Markets
San Andrecito, or 'Tourist Market', Vía 40. Where smuggled goods are sold at very competitive prices. Picturesque and reasonably safe. Any taxi driver will take you there.

Shopping centres
Centro Comercial Buenavista, Cra 53, C 98. Has a good selection of shops, cinemas and fast food outlets.

What to do

Barranquilla *p52, maps p52 and p53*

Tour operators
Aviatur, Cra 54, No 72-96, Edificio Miss Universo, local 3, T361 6000, www.aviatur.com.co. Organize tours to Parque Tayrona and other destinations.

Transport

Barranquilla *p52, maps p52 and p53*

Air
The bus to the airport (marked 'Malambo') leaves from Cra 44, goes up C 32 to C 38, and then C 30 to the airport.

Daily flights to **Bogotá**, **Cartagena**, **Medellín**, **Bucaramanga**, **Montería** and **Valledupar**. International flights to **Aruba**, **Curaçao**, **Miami** and **Panama City**.

Airline offices Avianca, Cra 56 No 75-155, local 102, T353 4989.

Bus
To **Santa Marta**, about 2 hrs, US$7.50, **Pullman** (less in non-a/c, Coolibertador), also direct to Santa Marta's Rodadero beach. To **Valledupar**, Copetran, 7 a day, 5-6 hrs, US$12.50. To **Montería** direct, 7-8 hrs, US$11. To **Medellín**, 16 hrs, US$40, **Pullman**. To **Bucaramanga**, frequent, 9 hrs, US$37.50 with **Copetran** (a/c, 1st class). To **Bogotá**, 5 a day, 20 hrs, US$40, direct with **Copetran**. To **Caucasia**, 8-11 hrs, US$17. To **Maicao**, every 30 mins from 0100-1200, 6 hrs, S$15, Brasilia and Copetran. To **Cartagena**, 2 hrs by *colectivo* US$7, 2½-3 hrs, US$4.50 with **Transportes Cartagena**; frequent, US$6 with **Copetran**; **Brasilia Van Tours** minibus, from their downtown offices and the bus terminals.

Taxi
To **Cartagena**, US$15 per person, leaves when full.

Directory

Barranquilla *p52, maps p52 and p53*

Embassies and consulates For your country's embassy or consulates in Colombia, see http://embassy.goabroad.com.
Security DAS, C 54, No 41-133, T371 7500; **Tourist police**, Cra 43, No 47-53, T351 0415, T340 9903.

Santa Marta and around

Santa Marta, the capital of Magdalena Department, is the third Caribbean port, 96 km east of Barranquilla. Unlike Cartagena, it is no colonial beauty but what it lacks in architecture it makes up for in character and bustle, and the Samarios are some of the most welcoming and gregarious people you will find anywhere in Colombia. The area around Santa Marta has much to offer, including a number of beaches. Head west to the family resort of Rodadero, or north to the former fishing village of Taganga. Backpackers love Taganga's lazy charm, it's a convenient stopping point en route to Tayrona and a good place to organize treks to Ciudad Perdida in the Sierra Nevada de Santa Marta. Southeast is Ciénaga de Santa Marta, 4000 sq km of wetlands with all types of waterbirds, and from here you can reach Aracataca, birthplace of Colombia's most famous writer, Gabriel García Márquez, and believed to be the inspiration for the village of Macondo which features in several of his books, including *One Hundred Years of Solitude*.

When leaving Santa Marta, most travellers will make a beeline for Tayrona National Park and its wild coastline of golden sands, secluded coves and tropical jungle. But there are other options. If the heat of the coast becomes too much, the rural village of Minca in the foothills of the Sierra Nevada, will provide welcome respite.

Arriving in Santa Marta
Getting there The airport, Simón Bolívar, is 20 km south of the city. A bus to town costs US$0.60 and a taxi to Santa Marta is US$10, or US$4 to Rodadero. If you arrive by bus, beware of taxi drivers who take you to a hotel of their choice, not yours. The bus terminal is southeast of the city, towards Rodadero, and a minibus to the centre of Santa Marta costs US$0.30, a taxi US$2.00. To Rodadero a taxi is US$4.

Although cruise ships from various places (eg USA, Puerto Rico, Panama and even Europe) visit Santa Marta from time to time, it is difficult to find a passage here from overseas. Without a *carnet de passages*, it can take up to four working days to get a car out of the port, but it is usually well guarded and it is unlikely that anything will be stolen.

Getting around Local bus services from Santa Marta to Rodadero cost US$0.60 (this is a flat fee all the way to the airport), and a taxi is US$4. Many of the buses coming from Barranquilla and Cartagena stop at Rodadero on their way to Santa Marta.

Tourist information The tourist office ① *Alcaldía Distrital de Santa Marta, C 14 No 2-49, T438 2777, turismo@santamarta.gov.co*. A useful website is www.santamartaturistica.org.

Climate This area is relatively humid but the on-shore winds moderate the temperature much of the time. February and March are pleasant months to visit.

Security The north end of town near the port and beyond the old railway station are dangerous and travellers are advised not to go there alone, as it's rife with drugs and prostitution is common. South of Rodadero beach has also been reported unsafe. Beware of jungle tours, or boat trips to the islands sold by street touts.

Background

This part of the South American coastline was visited in the early years of the 16th century by the new Spanish settlers from Venezuela. At this time, many indigenous groups were living on and near the coast, and were trading with each other and with communities further inland. The dominant group were the Tayrona.

Santa Marta was the first town created in Colombia by the conquistadors, in 1525. The founder, Rodrigo de Bastidas, chose it for its sheltered harbour and its proximity to the Río Magdelena and therefore its access to the hinterland. Also, the *indígenas* represented a potential labour force and he had not failed to notice the presence of gold in their ornaments.

Within a few years, the Spanish settlement was consolidated and permanent buildings appeared (see the Casa de la Aduana, below). Things did not go well, however. The *indígenas* did not 'collaborate' and there was continual friction amongst the Spaniards, all of whom were expecting instant riches. Bastidas' successor, Rodrigo Alvarez Palomino, attempted to subdue the *indígenas* by force, with great loss of life and little success. The *indígenas* that survived took to the hills and their successors, the Kogi, are still there today.

By the middle of the 16th century, a new threat had appeared. Encouraged and often financed by Spain's enemies (England, France and Holland), pirates realized that rich pickings were to be had, not only from shipping, but also by attacking coastal settlements. The first raid took place around 1544, captained by the French pirate Robert Waal with three ships and 1000 men. He was followed by many of the famous sea-dogs – the brothers Côte, Drake and Hawkins – who all ransacked the city in spite of the forts built on a small island at the entrance to the bay and on the mainland. Before the end of the century more than 20 attacks were recorded and the pillage continued until as late as 1779, the townsfolk living in constant fear. Cartagena, meanwhile, became the main base for the conquistadors and much was invested in its defences. Santa Marta was never fortified in the same way and declined in importance, something that accounts for a certain lack of colonial heritage here. Over the years caches of treasure have been unearthed in old walls and floors – testimonies to the men and women of those troubled times who did not survive to claim them.

Two important names connect Santa Marta with the history of Colombia. Gonzalo Jiménez de Quesada began the expedition here that led him up the Río Magdalena and into the highlands to found Santa Fe de Bogotá in 1538, and it was here that Simón Bolívar, his dream of Gran Colombia shattered, came to die. Almost penniless, he was given hospitality at the *quinta* of San Pedro Alejandrino, see below. He died there on 17 December 1830, at the age of 47.

Santa Marta → *Phone code: 5. Population: 385,000. For listings, see pages 67-72.*

Orientation

Santa Marta lies at the mouth of the Río Manzanares, one of the many rivers that drain the Sierra Nevada de Santa Marta, on a deep bay with high shelving cliffs at each end. The city's fine promenade offers good views of the bay and is lined with restaurants, accommodation and nightlife, though none of a very high quality. At the southern end, where the main traffic turns inland on Calle 22, is a striking sculpture dedicated to the indigenous heritage of the region, La Herencía Tairona. The main commercial area and banks are on Carrera 5 and Calle 15.

Places in Santa Marta

The centre of Santa Marta is the pleasant and leafy Plaza Bolívar, which leads down to the beach. It is complete with statues of Bolívar and Santander, and a bandstand. On the north side is the **Casa de la Aduana/Museo de Oro** ① *C 14/Cra 2*, which became the Custom House when Santa Marta was declared a free port in 1776. Previously it belonged to the Church and was used as the residence of the Chief Justice of the Inquisition.

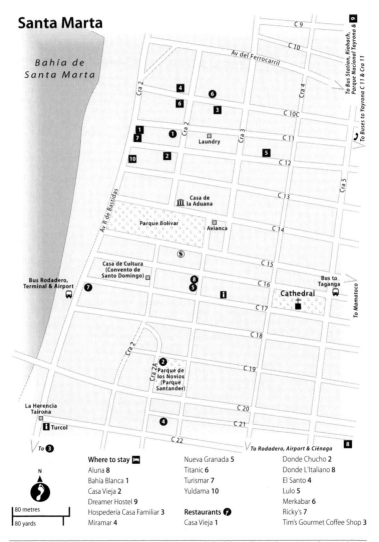

Santa Marta

Bahía de Santa Marta

To Bus Station, Ríohach, Parque Nacional Tayrona & 9
To Buses to Yayrona C 11 & Cra 11

Laundry

Casa de la Aduana

Parque Bolívar

Avianca

Casa de Cultura (Convento de Santo Domingo)

Bus Rodadero, Terminal & Airport

Cathedral

Bus to Taganga

To Mamatoco

Parque de los Novios (Parque Santander)

La Herencia Tairona

Turcol

To ❸

To Rodadero, Airport & Ciénaga

N

80 metres
80 yards

Where to stay	Restaurants	
Aluna **8**	Nueva Granada **5**	Donde Chucho **2**
Bahía Blanca **1**	Titanic **6**	Donde L'Italiano **8**
Casa Vieja **2**	Turismar **7**	El Santo **4**
Dreamer Hostel **9**	Yuldama **10**	Lulo **5**
Hospedería Casa Familiar **3**		Merkabar **6**
Miramar **4**	Restaurants ❼	Ricky's **7**
	Casa Vieja **1**	Tim's Gourmet Coffee Shop **3**

The house dates from 1531 and was probably the first built of brick and stone in Colombia. An upstairs garret, added in 1730, offers an excellent view of the city and the bay. Simón Bolívar stayed here briefly in December 1830 and he lay in state on the second floor from 17 December to the 20 December before being moved to the cathedral. The Custom House now displays an excellent archaeological collection, with four rooms of exhibits mainly dedicated to the indigenous Tayrona. Especially interesting is the model of Ciudad Perdida, the most important of the Tayrona cities. At the time of writing Casa de la Aduana was closed for conservation work, but it's still worth checking out its exterior. The **Museo de Oro** (**Gold Museum**) ① *usually contained within the building, has been moved to the library of Banco de la República next door, during the conservation work, Mon-Fri, 0830-1800, Sat 0900-1300, free*, with a number of pre-Columbian gold artefacts held in the vault.

Quinta de San Pedro Alejandrino ① *daily 0930-1700 (high season 0930-1800) US$5, discounts for students and children*, an early 17th-century villa, is 5 km southeast of the city and dedicated to sugar cane production. This is where Simón Bolívar lived out his last days and the simple room in which he died, with a few of his personal belongings, can be visited. Other paintings and memorabilia of the period are on display in the villa, and a contemporary art gallery featuring works by artists from Venezuela to Bolivia (the countries associated with Bolívar's life), and an exhibition hall have been built on the property. The estate and gardens, with some ancient cedars, *samanes*, dignified formal statues and monuments, can be visited. It is an impressive memorial to the man most revered by Colombians. To get there take a bus or *colectivo* from the waterfront, Carrera 1C, to Mamatoca and ask to be dropped off at the Quinta (US$0.60).

The original building on the site of the **cathedral** ① *Cra 4, C 16/17, open for Mass daily at 0600 and 1800 (more frequently on Sun), and you may find it open at 1000*, was completed a few years after the founding of the city and was probably the first church of Colombia as proclaimed by the inscription on the west front. The present building is mainly 17th century with many additions and modifications, hence the mixture of styles. There are interesting shrines along the aisles, a fine barrel roof and chandeliers, and a grey Italian marble altar decorated with red and brown, the whole giving a light, airy and dignified impression. Notable is the monument to Rodrigo de Bastidas, founder of the city, to the left of the main entrance and the inscription by the altar steps commemorating the period when Bolívar's remains rested here from his death in 1830 to 1842 when they were transferred to the Pantheon in Caracas. The **Convento de Santo Domingo** ① *Cra 2, No 16-44*, now serves as a cultural centre and houses a library.

Around Santa Marta → *For listings, see pages 67-72.*

There are rocky headlands and beaches in the bays and coves all along this coast, surrounded by hills, green meadows and shady trees. The largest sandy bay is that of Santa Marta, with Punta Betín, a promontory, protecting the harbour to the north and a headland to the south on top of which are the ruins of an early defensive fort, Castillo San Fernando. The rugged Isla El Morro lies 3 km off Santa Marta and is topped by a lighthouse. Because of the proximity of the port and the city, the beach is not recommended for bathing. There is marine ecosystem research science centre, run by Colombian and German universities near the end of Punta Betín.

In addition to those listed below, there are more beaches in the bays near the Cabo and Isla de la Aguja. Villa Concha has a nice beach, popular with the locals at the weekends and a good day trip during the week. The bay is surrounded by tree-covered hills and there are a number of restaurants nearby. ▶▶ *For further information on nearby beaches, see Tayrona National Park, page 62.*

Rodadero and around

Rodadero beach, 4 km southwest of Santa Marta, is one of the best along this coast. It is part of the municipality of **Gaira**, a small town 2 km away, alongside the main road, on the Río Gaira which flows into the Caribbean at the southern end of Rodadero beach. The main part of the beach has high rise hotels of all standards, but it is attractive, tree lined, relatively clean and pleasant for bathing. Behind the promenade are the restaurants, cheaper accommodation and services. Nearby are a number of holiday flats and other holiday centres operated by public and social entities. Rodadero is a popular destination for family holidays. There is a waterpark popular with kids and families at the southern end of the main beach (0900-1700, US$6). **Fondo de Promoción Turística** ① *C 10, No 3-10, T/F422 7548*, can provide local information and advice on hotels.

Launches leave Rodadero beach for the 10-minute trip to the **Aquarium**, north along the coast at Inca Inca Bay, where you'll find sharks, seals and many colourful fish of the Caribbean. The aquarium is linked to a small museum housing relics from Spanish galleons sunk by pirates, and a collection of coral and seashells. The boats leave from the beach at the end of Calle 12 every hour from 0800, the aquarium opens from 0900 and the

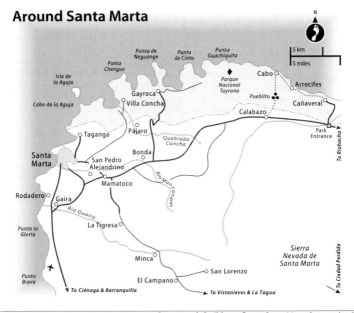

Around Santa Marta

N

Punta de Neguange
Punta de Cinto
Punta Guachiquita
Punta Chengue
5 km
5 miles
Isla de la Aguja
Parque Nacional Tayrona
Cabo
Arrecifes
Gayroca
Villa Concha
Pueblito
Cabo de la Aguja
Cañaveral
Calabazo
Taganga
Pájaro
Quebrada Concha
Park Entrance
Santa Marta
San Pedro Alejandrino
Bonda
Río Manzanares
Mamatoco
Rodadero
Gaira
Río Guaira
To Riohacha
Punta la Gloria
La Tigresa
Punta Brava
Minca
Sierra Nevada de Santa Marta
El Campano
San Lorenzo
To Ciénaga & Barranquilla
To Vistanieves & La Tagua
To Ciudad Perdida

last boat back leaves at 1630. Admission is US$7.50 and US$5 for children. **Coomarsertur** ① *T422 6208*, on the south end of the beach organizes boats US$5 per person (minimum four people) or US$4 per person (more than four people). From the aquarium, you can walk (10 minutes) to the Playa Blanca and swim in less crowded conditions than elsewhere. There is also food available at this beach.

Taganga and around

Close to Santa Marta is the former fishing village (most people now make a living from tourism) and beach of Taganga, 15-20 minutes away by minibus (US$0.50) or taxi (US$4). Set in a tranquil semi-circular bay surrounded by scorched hills dotted with cacti, Taganga attracts its fair share of backpackers and is fast changing from sleepy fishing village to more of a party resort. The swimming is good, especially on Playa Grande, 25 minutes' walk round the coast, but do not leave your belongings unattended. Taganga is even more popular at weekends. Boat trips along the coast for fishing, and to the many bays and beaches are run by **Hotel La Ballena Azul** and by a syndicate of boatmen along the beach.

Half an hour north of Taganga is Isla de la Aguja, a good fishing zone, and nearer is Playa Granate, with excellent places to snorkel and dive around the coral reefs, although lately the reefs have been showing signs of bleaching.

Ciénaga de Santa Marta

The paved coast road to Santa Marta from Barranquilla passes salt pans and skirts the Ciénaga de Santa Marta, where all types of waterbirds, plants and animals may be seen. Cutting off the access to the sea to build the coast road caused an ecological disaster, but a National Environment Programme has been working to restore the area. There are several villages built on stilts in the lake. On the east shore of the lagoon is **Ciénaga**, famous for *cumbia* music.

Aracataca

Aracataca, 60 km south of Ciénaga and 7 km before Fundación, is the birthplace of Gabriel García Márquez. It was fictionalized as Macondo in some of his novels, notably in *One Hundred Years of Solitude*. His home is now a modest museum 1½ blocks from the plaza, ask for directions. There are *residencias*, try **Hospedaje El Porvenir**, and a restaurant, but it is better to stay in Fundación. In 2007 a new train was inaugurated, **El Tren Amarillo de Macondo**, between Santa Marta and Aracataca. García Márquez himself, with a large entourage, joined the first run on 30 May 2007; however, a regular service has yet to come into operation.

Parque Nacional Tayrona → *For listings, see pages 67-72.*

The beaches of Tayrona National Park are what you would expect of a tropical paradise; thick jungle teeming with wildlife spills over onto golden sand beaches with pounding surf and there are small, secluded bays, excellent for swimming and sunbathing. There is something of the prehistoric about Tayrona. Squint your eyes and with a little imagination the flocks of pelicans that glide overhead become pterodactyls, the bright-tailed lizards that scurry underfoot as you walk through the forest paths reminders of their extinct cousins and the enormous boulders that stand guard over the beaches look like they have

Gabriel García Márquez

More than any other Colombian, Gabriel García Márquez, or Gabo as he is affectionately known, has shaped the outside world's understanding of Colombian culture. His books champion the genre of magical realism where the real and the fantastical blur so naturally that it is difficult to discern where one ends and the other begins.

But is this what life in Colombia is really like? Schoolteachers-turned-dictators who fashion a town's children into an oppressive army, a woman so beautiful she causes the death of anyone who courts her and a child born with his eyes open because he has been weeping in his mother's womb seem improbable, especially to sceptical Western sensibilities. Yet many of the places, events and characters are based on real life. Macondo, a place which features in so many of his stories, is modelled on his town of birth, Aracataca. Cartagena is easily recognizable as the unnamed port that is the setting for *Love in the Time of Cholera*, while Fermina Daza and Florentino Ariza's love affair is based on his own parents' marriage. Events in *Chronicle of a Death Foretold* and *The Story of a Shipwrecked Sailor* were inspired by real life stories lifted from newspaper articles.

"Owing to his hands-on experience in journalism, García Márquez is, of all the great living authors, the one who is closest to everyday reality", wrote the American literary critic Gene H Bell-Villada, and who can challenge Gabo's interpretation of the truth when Colombia has produced real life characters such as Pablo Escobar? Where else in the world are there villages that host donkey beauty contests or elect a mayor who dresses up as a superhero? Sometimes Colombian reality is stranger than Gabo's fiction.

been there since the beginning of time. However, time and tourism have caught up with Tayrona and it is becoming increasingly popular. Prices have rocketed in the past 10 years and there is now a steady stream of visitors, especially during national holidays. If you want to enjoy this corner of paradise in isolation then you might consider avoiding the busier periods of Semana Santa, July, August and December to January.

The park is named after the Tayrona (also spelt Tairona) culture, one of the most important of pre-colonial Colombia. It extends from north of Taganga for some 85 km of rugged coastline much of it fringed with coral reefs. You will see monkeys, iguanas and maybe snakes.

Arriving in Parque Nacional Tayrona

Getting there To get to the park entrance, take a minibus from the **market** ⓘ *Cra 11/ C 11*, in Santa Marta. The services are frequent and start from 0700, with the last minibus back at 1730 or later, but double check. The journey will take 45 minutes and cost about US$2. Alternatively, go to the Riohacha road police checkpoint (taxi US$1 or bus to Mamatoca) and catch any bus there going towards Riohacha. Private minivan can also be organized at hotels or with tour operators, approximately US$6 per person depending on number of passengers.

Park information Entry to the park is US$17.50 per person, US$3 for a motorcycle, US$4.50 for a car. Open 0800-1700. If you arrive before 0800, you may be able to pay at the car park at Cañaveral. Visitors normally stay overnight and hotels can help with arranging tours. Normally, you are advised to book accommodation before going, especially at holiday times. However, in the past few years, the park has been closed for safety, water shortages, local staffing and other reasons, only to be reopened after a short break. Unfortunately, this has given rise to confusion and contradiction. The best place for information is Santa Marta, and hopefully you will find that the park is open when you wish to visit. Information can also be found on the **Colombian Tourist Board – Proexport's** website, www.colombia.travel.

Hiking boots may be useful and there are sometimes bloodsucking insects to contend with. There are by now food and water stands available in the park, or you can take your own food and water, but no valuables as robbery has been a problem. You can hire horses to carry you and your luggage from Cañaveral to Arrecifes (US$8) and El Cabo de San Juan (US$18). Littering was a big problem in the past, but there are now camouflaged litter bins along all the main trails and around the campsites. In the wet, the paths are very slippery. There is no need to take guides, who charge US$20 or more per person, for a day trip.

Out of high season the park is relatively empty and you will usually find beaches with barely a soul on them. But beware, during holiday periods, especially during Semana Santa, the visitor numbers can increase fivefold.

Around the park

There are various places where there is access to the bays and beaches by road, including an unsurfaced road from the eastern edge of Santa Marta at Bastidas north 5 km to the beach at Villa Concha (see below). On towards Riohacha beyond Bonda there is a road in poor condition to Bahía Gayraca and Neguange (where indigenous peoples had an important settlement to exploit marine salt resources), to a point near Ancón Cinto. You can reach Negangue beach by *colectivo* from Santa Marta. Enquire also for transport to Villa Concha. Alternatively, take a boat from Taganga.

The normal entry to the park is further on, turning off the main road at El Zaino, 35 km from Santa Marta and at the eastern end of the park. From there, a road leads within the park 4 km to the administrative and visitor centre with car park at **Cañaveral**, about one hour's walk into the park from the gate. About 40 minutes west of Cañaveral on foot is **Arrecifes**, from where it is a 45-minute walk to El Cabo de San Juan, then up inland along a stream (La Boquita) 1½ hours on a clear path to the archaeological site of **Pueblito**. A guided tour around the site is free, but check at the entry if it is available. There are many other smaller Tayrona settlements in the park area and relics abound. At Pueblito there are indigenous people; do not photograph them without permission. From Pueblito you can either return to Cañaveral, or continue for a pleasant two-hour walk to Calabazo on the Santa Marta–Riohacha road. A circuit of Santa Marta, Cañaveral, Arrecifes, Pueblito, Calabazo, Santa Marta in one day is arduous, needing an early start.

Bathing is not recommended near Cañaveral or Arrecifes as there is often heavy pounding surf and the currents are treacherous. About 5 km east of Cañaveral are splendid, deserted sandy beaches. You have to walk there, but take care as the park borders marijuana-growing areas. The beach at **Villa Concha** is one of the most beautiful beaches of the area, with camping and several places to eat. Beyond Arrecifes (the sea can be dangerous on this beach) near **Cabo de San Juan** is La Piscina, a beautiful, safe natural swimming pool, excellent for snorkelling. Other safe bathing beaches can be found further along the shore but the going is difficult.

East from Tayrona
Approximately 3 km beyond Cañaveral and Guachaca along the coast is **Los Angeles** ① *Km 33.5 on the Santa Marta–Riohacha road*, a camping site which offers access to fine empty beaches, excellent for surfing, at a fraction of the cost of a stay in Tayrona. Charming owner Nohemi Ramos hires out hammocks or tents for around US$10 (less if you bring your own) and can cook up simple meals of freshly caught fish. She also offers guided tours of Tayrona, Pueblito and other local sights (for Spanish speakers, and she can put you in touch with English-speaking guides).

A 10-minute walk west from Los Angeles brings you to the mouth of the Río Piedras, the border of Tayrona Park, where you can bathe in the company of egrets and enjoy sights to rival any of those seen in the park. The paved coastal road continues from Tayrona and crosses into Guajira Department at Palomino, 80 km from Santa Marta, which has a fine beach and cheap *cabañas* as accommodation; 72 km from Palomino is Los Camarones and the entry to Santuario Los Flamencos, 25 km short of Riohacha.

Ciudad Perdida → *For listings, see pages 67-72.*

Ciudad Perdida (Lost City) is the third of the triumvirate of 'must-sees' on Colombia's Caribbean coast (the other two being Cartagena and Tayrona). The six-day trek is right up there with the Inca Trail in Peru and Roraima in Venezuela, as one of the classic South American adventures and is a truly memorable experience.

Don't forget that Ciudad Perdida is in a national park: it is strictly forbidden to damage trees and collect flowers or insects. Note also that there are over 1200 steps to climb when you get there.

The site
Discovered as recently as 1975, Cuidad Perdida was founded near the Río Buritaca between 500 and 700 AD and was surely the most important centre of the Tayrona culture. It stands at 1100 m on the steep slopes of Cerro Corea, which lies in the northern part of the Sierra Nevada de Santa Marta. The site, known as Teyuna to the indigenous locals, covers 400 ha and consists of a complex system of buildings, paved footpaths, flights of steps and perimetrical walls, which link a series of terraces and platforms, on which were built cult centres, residences and warehouses. Juan Mayr's book, *The Sierra Nevada of Santa Marta* (Mayr y Cabal, Bogotá), deals beautifully with Ciudad Perdida.

Trekking
Five or six-day trips can be organized by the tourist office and Turcol in Santa Marta (see page 71). Price should include transport, mules and porters, guide and food, but double check that you don't need to pay extra for porters. It is three days there, one day (two nights) at the site, and two days back. The route goes beyond Parque Tayrona on the road to Riohacha, then past Guachaca turning inland to the roadhead at El Mamey. The climb

The Lost City

From the first day we set out on the trail toward the mysterious Colombian Lost City, until day six when the remarkable adventure into the heart of the sierra came to an end, I was blown away by the crystal-clear rivers that cascaded down from the upper reaches of the mountains and treated us to amazing natural swimming pools, beautiful waterfalls and a much welcomed respite after hours of hiking amidst the endless jungle landscape. There are 18 or so river crossings en route to the Lost City, river pools to swim in each day and 1300 stone steps to climb at the very end of the third day that take you above the gorgeous river valleys to the high ridges blanketed in green. While the site alone is impressive, and its mysterious history and late discovery only add to its splendour, the surrounding mountain peaks dominate the endless landscape. What else lies undiscovered and hidden among such wild, rugged and beautiful terrain?

Despite the unsettling events in 2003, when eight foreigners were kidnapped along the Lost City trail, the region is currently considered safe and is heavily patrolled by the Colombian Army. The site is guarded day and night by about 40 friendly soldiers who pass their two month assignment on site by asking visitors for cigarettes in exchange for odd looking nuts that they have picked up off the jungle floor. They will also obligingly pose for photos, which they seem to enjoy more than anything else.

There is more than one option when it comes to choosing a route, some a little more difficult and with longer days, but the rewards will outweigh the fatigue. Starting and finishing the hike in different places will give you the chance to see more of the remote landscape and travel to less visited parts of this unique mountain range. For more information on trekking, see page 65.

Craig Weigand

broadly follows the Río Buritaca, and apart from crossing a number of streams, is uphill all the way. Ciudad Perdida is on a steep slope overlooking Río Buritaca.

Ask at hotels in Santa Marta (eg **Hotel Miramar**) or Taganga, or at the Santa Marta market for alternative tours. If you are prepared to shop around, and cook and carry your supplies and belongings, a tour could cost you less. Under no circumstances should you deal with unauthorized guides, check with the tourist office if in doubt, and try to get views of the quality of guides from travellers who have already done the trip.

You will need to take a tent or a hammock and mosquito net (on organized tours these may be supplied by the guide), a good repellent, sleeping bag, warm clothing for the night, torch, plastic bags to keep everything dry, and strong, quick-drying footwear. Small gifts for the indigenous children are appreciated.

Be prepared for heavy rain – the northern slopes of the Sierra Nevada have an average rainfall of over 4000 mm per year. Check conditions, especially information on river crossings, and ensure you have adequate food, a water bottle and water purifying tablets before you start. Try to leave no rubbish behind and encourage the guides to ensure no one else does. Going on your own is discouraged and dangerous. Route finding is very difficult and unwelcoming *indígenas*, paramilitaries and drug traders increase the hazards. Properly organized groups appear to be safe.

Sierra Nevada de Santa Marta → *For listings, see pages 67-72.*

Minca

ⓘ *Catch a bus from C 11 with Cra 11 in Santa Marta (30 mins, US$1.50). A taxi will cost US$10.*

If the heat of the coast becomes too much then a stay up in Minca is a refreshing alternative. Some 20 km from Santa Marta in the foothills of the Sierra Nevada, this small village, surrounded by coffee *fincas* and begonia plantations, is becoming increasingly popular and offers several cheap and truly charming places to stay. Horse riding, birdwatching and tours further into the Sierra Nevada can be arranged from here.

About 45 minutes walk beyond the village is **El Pozo Azul**, a local swimming spot under a waterfall, popular at weekends but almost always empty during the week, well worth a visit. El Pozo Azul was a a sacred indigenous site where purification rituals were performed and on occasion it is still used by the Kogi of the Sierra Nevada.

San Lorenzo

Beyond Minca, the partly paved road rises steeply to San Lorenzo which is surrounded by a forest of palm trees. On the way to San Lorenzo is **La Victoria**, a large coffee *finca* which offers tours to demonstrate the coffee-making process. It is possible to stay in *cabañas* run by the park authorities near San Lorenzo. **Aventure Colombia** organizes tours with guides, transportation, food and lodging to this section of the park.

☺ Santa Marta and around listings → *Phone code: 5.*

For sleeping and eating price codes and other relevant information, see pages 8-13.

● Where to stay

Santa Marta *p58, map p59*
Av Rodrigo de Bastidas (Cra 1) has several seafront holiday hotels while **Cra 2** and connecting *calles* have many budget *residencias*. For groups of 4 or more, consider short-let apartments. All hotels near the beach can be noisy, especially at weekends.
$$ Hotel Bahía Blanca, Cra 1, 11-12, T423 6411. Slightly impersonal, but with a pleasant patio serving breakfast. Right near the beach and all the action.
$$ Hotel Casa Vieja, C 12, No 1-58, T431 1606, www.hotelcasavieja.com. Has a Spanish feel about it with white tiling and simple, clean rooms and a/c. Prices cheaper with fan. Friendly staff and a pleasant restaurant serving delicious Colombian food.
$$ Nueva Granada, C 12, No 3-17, T421 1337, www.hotelnuevagranada.com.

This charming old building in the historic quarter has a peaceful courtyard and a yacuzzi pool. Breakfast is served in the pleasant patio, they have bikes for guests to borrow and offer welcome drinks, airport transfers, a medical service and free calls to the US and Canada. The pick of the bunch. Highly recommended.
$$ Yuldama, Cra 1, No 12-19, on the seafront, T421 0063, www.hotel yuldama.com. Modern but a bit sterile, with clean rooms, a/c, cable TV, Wi-Fi and safe provided.
$ Aluna, C 21 5-72, T432 4916, www.aluna hotel.com. Irish-run, pleasant, large hostel with private rooms and a dorm with roof terrace. Kitchen, laundry service, Wi-Fi, new café and a good noticeboard. Recommended.
$ Dreamer Hostel, Cra 51, No 26D, 161 Los Trupillos, Mamatoco, T300-251 6534, www.thedreamerhostel.com. Newish hostel, opened in Dec 2009, just 5 mins from the bus station.

$ Hospedería Casa Familiar, C 10C, No 2-14, T421 1697, www.hospederia casafamiliar. freeservers.com. An extremely friendly and helpful family run this hostel. Offers rooms with a private bath and fan, dorms and space for hammocks. Pleasant roof terrace and kitchen available. Has its own dive shop and organizes trips to Tayrona and Ciudad Perdida. Recommended.

$ Hotel Titanic, C 10C, No 1C-68, T421 1947. Opposite the **Miramar**, offering similar rooms with own bath, fan and cable TV. Clean but a little dark.

$ Miramar, C 10C, No 1C-59, T423 3276. Its reputation as the ultimate backpackers' hotel precedes it. Basic but cheap rooms, a good restaurant serving delicious fruit juices, has a number of computers and Wi-Fi, and organizes tours to Tayrona Park and Ciudad Perdida.

$ Turismar, Cra 1a, No 11-41, T421 2408. A good option for a dorm but individual rooms are dark and spartan. Beachside, with pleasant courtyard and newly opened restaurant.

Rodadero *p61*

$$$$ Tamacá, Cra 2, No 11A-98, T422 7016, www.tamaca.com. Resort-style hotel with fine pool, casino, large reception area and direct access to beach. All rooms have balcony with sea view, hot water, Wi-Fi and a safe but are a little sterile. Half- and full-board also available.

$$$ Hotel La Sierra, Cra 1, No 9-47, T422 7960, www.hotelasierra.com. Fine hotel with pleasant terrace set back from beach, rooms with balcony and Wi-Fi. Recommended.

$$$-$$ El Rodadero, C 11, No 1-29, T422 8323, www.hopertour.com. Stylish, modern building with a touch of art deco. Excellent pool, rooms with fine views of the beach and breakfast and dinner included.

$$ Hotel Bariloche, C 13, No 2-59, 500 m from the beach, T422 8692, hotelbariloche77 @hotmail.com. Leafy, tiled courtyard with fountain. Rooms are clean but a little musty.

$$ Hotel Nashama, C 13, No 2-41, T422 5794. Clean but unspectacular rooms, with a/c and TV. There is a restaurant and they offer discounts for groups.

$$ Tucuraca, Cra 2, No 12-43, 2 mins' walk from the beach, T422 7493, hoteltucuraca@ yahoo.com. Rooms are clean with cable TV and a/c or fan, but lacking character. Wi-Fi available. For groups of 4 or more, ask for apartments.

Taganga *p62*

$$$ La Ballena Azul, Cra 1, No 18-01, T421 9009, www.hotelballenaazul.com. Right on the beach, this stylish hotel offers friendly service, a fine restaurant and a terrace bar. Decorated in cool blues and whites, rooms open onto a central atrium with hanging bougainvillea and a palm tree. If you are prepared to spend a little more this is easily the best option in town. Rooms with fan or a/c, breakfast included, Wi-Fi available.

$$ Bahía Taganga, C 4 No 1B-35, T421 9049, www.bahiataganga.com. If you want to get away from the backpacker crowd and can't afford **La Ballena Azul**, then this is your place. Up on a hill at the north end of the bay it has commanding views over the village and is tastefully decorated with clean rooms. Friendly owner.

$ Bayview Hostel, Cra 4, No 17B-57, T421 9560, www.bayviewhostel.com. With a technicolour façade, it offers pleasant rooms with balconies or cheaper dorms with bunk beds. There's a kitchen, BBQ area, 2 lounges with DVD player and rocking chairs, and Wi-Fi.

$ Casa Blanca, Cra 1, No 18-161, at the southern end of the beach, www.casablanca hosteltaganga.com. Crumbling but has character. Each room has a balcony with hammock and the roof terrace is a fine place to pass the evening drinking beer with fellow guests.

$ Casa de Felipe, Cra 5A, No 19-13, 500 m from beach behind football field, T421 9101, www.lacasadefelipe.com. The true backpackers' choice. Has a shady garden of bougainvillea, cacti and hammocks, its own kitchen and Wi-Fi. Some dorms available.

$pp Divanga B&B, C 12, No 4-07, T421 9092, and also **Casa Divanga** C 11 No 3-05, T421 9217, www.divanga.com. French-owned hostels, doubles with private bath or 3-person dorm, includes great breakfast, comfortable, 5-mins' walk from beach, nice views, attentive service, lovely atmosphere, good pool, HI affiliated, Wi-Fi, internet. Recommended.

$ Hostal Moramar, Cra 4, No-17B-83, T421 9202, www.hostalmoramar.com. 2 blocks up from beach opposite football pitch. Simple, quiet rooms with bath and fan, bright, airy, patio, laundry, attentive owners, welcoming.

$ Hotel Pelikan, Cra 2, No 17-04, T421 9057. Has character and offers rooms with fan and private bath. Laundry service available.

$ Techos Azules, Sector Dunkarinca, Cabaña 1-100, T421 9141, www.techosazules.com. Off the road leading into town, this hostel is a collection of *cabañas* with good views over the bay. Offers internet, free coffee and a laundry service.

Parque Nacional Tayrona *p62*

Thatched 'eco' *cabañas* (**$$$$**) are available in the park, they are circular cabins built in the style of indigenous *bohíos*, which hold 2-6 people. These cost at least US$300 in high season for 2-4 people, US$240 in low season, and the price includes breakfast, cable TV, phone, safe and hot water. There is also a spa offering various massages and treatments. The eco refers more to proximity to nature than any strict environmental policy, although they do recycle. Great views over sea and jungle and a good restaurant.

Park accommodation in Arrecifes and Cañaveral is managed by Aviatur, C 15, No 3-20, T421 3848, reservasparques@ aviatur.com.co, T01-900-331 2222/01-382 1616, or Bogotá, T381 7111. National parks office: C 17, No 4-06, Santa Marta, T421 1732.

Camping Campsite US$15 for a 5-person tent, or US$4 for a hammock. There are

facilities, but only a tiny shop, take all supplies or eat in the restaurant. An attractive site but plenty of mosquitoes. Beware of falling coconuts and omnivorous donkeys.

Arrecifes

$$$$ Yuluca, Arrecifes beach. Huts with TV, safe, minibar, fan and ultra sonic insect repellent. US$225 for 2-4 people in high season; US$170 in low season.

Camping Yuluca (see above) charges around US$3 for a tent, US$8 for a hammock, and offers fresh water showers and toilets, very clean. There is a good restaurant, though bringing your own food is recommended, as it is expensive.

Cabo de San Juan

Camping On the path to Pueblito, there is a campsite at this beautiful double bay divided by a thin strip of sand and a large rock, where there is excellent bathing. There is also a small restaurant and hammocks for hire (US$13 in high season or US$10 in low season); there are 2 *cabañas* built on the rock that divides the 2 bays (US$50 in high season or US$43 in low season); pitching your own tent will set you back US$7, while hiring a tent for 2 persons costs US$19. There are other camping and hammock places en route. There is nowhere to stay at Pueblito.

Minca *p67*

$$ Sierra's Sound, C Principal, T421 9993, www.sierrasound.es.tl. With a veranda overlooking a rocky river, pasta home made by its Italian owner, hot water, TV and organized tours into the Sierra Nevada, this is perhaps the most sophisticated place to stay in Minca.

$ La Casona, on the hill to the right as you enter the village, T421 9958, lacasona@ colombiaexotic.com. With commanding views of the valley below, this is a converted convent with a wraparound veranda. The

art is by the owner, a sculptor from Bogotá, who runs the hostel with his family. Magical.
$ Sans Souci, T421 9968, sanssouciminca@yahoo.com. Rambling house in beautiful garden of bamboo and exotic flowers. German owner Chris provides rooms in the house or separate apartments. Has rustic swimming pool, football pitch, kitchen and the option of a discount in exchange for gardening services. Stunning views.

🍴 Restaurants

Santa Marta *p58, map p59*
$$$-$$ El Santo, C 21 2A-52. Gorgeous Argentine food with happy hour 1700-2000, 2x1 *mojitos*.
$$ Donde Chucho, C 19 2-17. A little expensive but well situated in the corner of Parque Santander (Parque de los Novios). Serves seafood and pasta.
$$ Donde l'Italiano, next door to Lulo, serves up tasty Italian fare at reasonable prices. Generous portions. Recommended.
$$ Ricky's, Cra 1a, No 17-05. Beachside restaurant serving international food, including Chinese. Reasonably priced.
$ Lulo, Cra 3 16-34, www.lulocafebar.com. Cosy café and bar in the pedestrianized part of Cra 3. Organic coffee, fresh juices and gourmet *arepas*.
$ Merkabar, C 10C, No 2-11. Pastas, great pancakes, good juices and specializes in seafood. Also open early for good breakfasts. Family-run, good value and provides tourist information. Recommended.
$ Restaurante Casa Vieja, C 12, No 1-58. Part of the hotel, see Where to stay. Serves delicious *comida criolla*.
$ Tim's Gourmet Coffee Shop, Cra 1A 23-57, behind the marina, www.tims gourmetcoffee. Com. Colombian/Canadian-run café open 7 days a week 0700-2000, serving great coffee, crêpes and sandwiches, fresh fruit juices and Canadian desserts. Has Wi-Fi. Recommended.

Rodadero *p61*
There are fast-food restaurants and very good juice kiosks along the seafront. Cra 2 between C 7 and 8 has a food court, serving everything from pizzas and Mexican, to Colombian grilled meats (*asados*) and there is a Chinese next door. The same stretch also has a number of bars and discos.
$ El Banano, Cra 2, No 7-38. Good meat dishes and light meals, try their *carne asada con maduro* (banana) *y queso crema*, delicious. Recommended.
$ El Pibe, C 6, No 1-26. Argentine-run restaurant, serving steaks.

Taganga *p62*
Fresh fish is available along the beach and good pancakes can be found at the crêperie at the **Hotel La Ballena Azul**.
$ Bitácora, Cra 4, No 17-03, just off the beach. Serves seafood, pastas, burgers, steaks and salads.
$ Donde Juanita, Cra 1, No 17-1. Serves fine home-cooked food, including fish and meat. Very cheap, with good vegetarian options.
$ Yiu Nu Sagu, C 12, No 1-08. Beachside pizzeria, large helpings.

🍸 Bars and clubs

Santa Marta *p58, map p59*
Santa Marta is a party town; new clubs, discos and bars open every week. The website www.samarios.com, is an excellent resource for finding out what's going on at night.
Barrio Samario, C 17 No 3-36, between Cra 3 and 4 (on same road as **La Puerta**). A popular bar playing local music.
La Puerta, C 17 No 2-29, between Cra 3 and 4. Excellent bar and atmosphere in a colonial house. Highly recommended.

Rodadero *p61*
There are many bars and nightclubs here.
Burukuka, Vía al Edif Cascadas del Rodadero, T301-374 6620, www.burukuka.com. Steak bar looking out over Rodadero beach.

La Escollera, Cra 4 and C 5, No 4-107, www.la-escollera.com. Huge club under an open straw roof. Concerts are also staged here.

Taganga *p62*
El Garaje, C 8 No 2-127 with Cra 3, T421 9003. Plays hip hop and other forms of electronic music. Starts late, finishes late.
Mojito Net, C 14, No 1B-61. Open 0800-0200, happy hour 1400-2100. Live music, open-mic sessions, wine, cocktails, food and internet.

✹ Festivals

Santa Marta *p58, map p59*
Jul Festival Patronal de Santa Marta. Celebrates the founding of the city with parades and musical performances.
Jul Fiestas del Mar Aquatic events and a beauty contest.
Sep International Caribbean Theatre Festival. Contributions from many of the Caribbean countries.

◎ Shopping

Santa Marta *p58, map p59*
Look around for small artefacts and figurines in the indigenous tradition, sometimes sold on the beach. Best if you can find the artists who live in and around Santa Marta.

Craft shops
The market is at C 11/Cra 11, just off Av del Ferrocarril and has stalls with excellent selections of hammocks. There are several good handicraft shops on Parque Bolívar.
Artesanías La 15, C15 with Cra 9, T310 730 9606, good selection of typical handicrafts;
Artesanías Sisa, Cra 4, No 16-42 on the Plaza Catedral, T421 4510, local handicrafts including bags, hammocks and sombreros;
José Pertuz, C 38, up the hill beyond Cra 17.

Shopping malls
El Barco, C 13, No 5-26; **El Emporio**, C 12 No 8-105.

⚠ What to do

Santa Marta *p58, map p59*
For guided trips to Quinta San Pedro Alejandrino and other local points of interest, ask at your hotel, travel agencies or the tourist office. Similarly, if you wish to visit the Marine Centre at Punta Betín you will need a boat or a permit to pass through the port area, so ask for guidance. For trips to Tayrona National Park, Ciudad Perdida and the Sierra Nevada, see under the relevant destination. Coach tours also go to Aracataca and Ciénaga de Santa Marta from Santa Marta.

Tour operators
Aviatur, C 15, No 3-20, T421 3848. Good service.
New Frontiers Adventures, Calle 27, No 1C- 74 (close to Playa los Cocos), T317-648 6786, www.colombia.new frontiersadventures.com. Arranges trips with English-speaking guides to the Ciudad Perdida, Tayrona National Park and Guajira.
Nohemi Ramos, Tierra Mar Aire, C 15, No 2-60, T421 5161. Amex agent and full tourist travel agent.
Sendero Tairona, Cra 3, No 18-46, T422 9505, clubsenderotayrona@gmail.com. A hiking club, offers trips into Tayrona Park and the Sierra Nevada from US$130, which includes transport, food, guides and accommodation.
Turcol, Cra 1C, No 20-15, T/F421 2256, www.buritaca2000.com. Arranges trips and provides a guide service.

Rodadero *p61*

Diving shops
Caribbean Divers, Cra 1, No 5-113, Local 1, Edif Rodamar, T422 0878, www.caribbean diverscol.com. Offers PADI and NAUI qualifications. A mini course costs US$90.

Taganga *p62*

Diving shops
There are various dive shops in Taganga.
Aquantis, B&B and Diving, C 18, No 1-39,
T316-818 4285, www.aquantis
center.com. Belgian-run, PADI-certified,
passionate team, PADI course US$275.
Recommended.
Oceano Scuba, Cra 2, No 17-46, T421 9004,
www.oceanoscuba.com.co. PADI courses,
2, 3 and 4 days from US$70.
Octopus Diving Center, C 15, No 1B-14,
T317-327 7570, www.octopusdivecenter
taganga.com. PADI, NAUI and BIS courses.
Night and wreck dives offered. English spoken.
Poseidon Dive Center, C 18, No 1-69,
T421 9224, www.poseidondivecenter.com.
PADI courses at all levels and the only place
on the Colombian Caribbean coast to offer
an instructor course. Offers a tourist package
with no sales tax. German owner, with
English and Croatian spoken. Own pool
for beginners, also has rooms to rent.
Tayrona Dive Center, Cra 2, No 18A-22,
T318-305 9589, www.tayronadivecenter.com.
Mini course with 2 dives is US$77.

Parque Nacional Tayrona *p62*
Ecoturt come highly recommended for
guided tours of Pueblito and other parts
of the park. Speak to Nohemi Ramos or
Jarven Rodríguez, T316-373 8846, ecoturt@
latinmail.com. Some English spoken.

Ciudad Perdida *p67*
Expotur Eco, C 18 No 2A-07, T421 9493,
www.expotur-eco.com. Community tourism
and Ciudad Perdida treks from US$250 for
6 days.
Magic Tour Taganga, T421 9429/5820,
www.magictourstaganga.com. Offices
in Santa Marta and Taganga. Work
closely with **La Ballena Azul**.

○ Transport

Santa Marta *p58, map p59*

Air
There are daily flights to **Bogotá** and
Medellín, as well as connections to other
cities. During the tourist season get to the
airport early and book well ahead (the
same goes for bus reservations). Facilities
at the airport are sparse, no exchange
or internet, but a reasonable restaurant
on the ground floor.
   Airline offices Avianca, Cra 2A
No 14-17, Edif de los Bancos, Local 105,
T421 4958, T432 0106 at airport; Centro
Comercial Prado Plaza, Cra 4, No 26-40,
T431 2020; and at C 7, Cra 3 esq, Edif Los
Andes, Rodadero T422 7211.

Bus
To **Barranquilla**, 7 daily, 2 hrs, US$5.50,
Brasilia, 3 daily with Copetran, US$10. To
Medellín, 6 daily, 15 hrs, US$52, Brasilia or
Copetran. To **Bogotá**, 7 daily, 16 hrs, US$45,
Brasilia or Copetran. To **Cartagena**, 5 hrs,
US$12.50, Copetran. To **Riohacha**, 3 hrs,
US$8.50. Frequent buses to **Maicao**, 4-5 hrs,
US$12.50 for a/c or cheaper for buses
without. Brasilia runs a bus through to
Maracaibo, daily, US$28. To **Bucaramanga**,
9 hrs, US$35, Brasilia or Copetran. To
Mompós there's a door to door *colectivo*
service, US$30 with Asotranstax, C 23, No 4-27.

Sea
Although cruise ships stop here, it is difficult
to find onward passage.

● Directory

Santa Marta *p58, map p59*
Emergencies Police, T112.
Immigration DAS Office,
Cra 8, No 26A-15, T421 4917.

East to Venezuela

Along the coast from Santa Marta the lush vegetation of the foothills of the Sierra Nevada gives way to flat expanses of scorched earth where only a scrub-like tree known as trupillo and the cactus survive. The change in landscape marks the beginning of the Guajira Peninsula, home to the Wayúu. It is also the northernmost tip of South America and it certainly feels like the end of the world; an arid and unforgiving terrain which nonetheless offers a home to vast flocks of flamingos and other birds and a chance to mingle with one of Colombia's best-preserved indigenous cultures. Riohacha may be a departmental capital but it feels more like a sleepy fishing village, though it livens up considerably at the weekend and on public holidays. Musichi and Manaure with their flocks of flamingos and salt works will be of interest to nature lovers and Cabo de la Vela with its turquoise waters that lap against a desert landscape is a sight to behold. If you have the time and energy then Parque Natural Nacional Macuira, an oasis of tropical green sprouting out of the semi desert, and Punta Gallinas, the northernmost point of the continent, will cap off a trip into this strange and sometimes ethereal land. The difficulties in transport only add to the sense of adventure this peninsula presents.

Riohacha → *For listings, see pages 78-81. Population: 169,000*

Riohacha, 160 km east of Santa Marta, is capital of La Guajira Department. Formerly a port, today it has the ambience of a provincial fishing town. The city was founded in 1545 by Nicolás Federmann. One of Riohacha's resources of those days was oyster beds, and the pearls were valuable enough to tempt Drake to sack it. Pearling almost ceased during the 18th century and the town was all but abandoned. José Prudencio Padilla, who was born here, was in command of the Republican fleet that defeated the Spaniards in the Battle of Lago Maracaibo in 1823. He is buried in the **cathedral**, and there is a statue in the central park which bears his name. *Riohacha y Los Indios Guajiros*, by Henri Candelier, a Frenchman's account of a journey to the area 100 years ago, has very interesting depictions of the life of the Wayúu.

The **José Prudencio Padilla Airport** is south of the town towards Tomarrazón and the main **bus terminal** is on Calle 15 (Avenida El Progreso)/Carrera 11. There are good white-sand beaches lined with coconut palms and a long wooden pier in the centre. Also two bustling markets, the old market in town and a newer one further out, are worth a visit. At weekends Riohacha fills up, with bars and music springing up all over the place. The sea is clean, despite the dark silt stirred up by the waves and it is a good place to take stock before pushing through into the more remote areas of La Guajira. There is a tourist office, **Dirección de Turismo de Guajira** ① *Cra 7/C 1, Av La Marina, T727 1015*, which is well organized.

Santuario Los Flamencos

① *US$17 entry fee for non-nationals.*
The Santuario de Fauna y Flora Los Flamencos is 7000 ha of saline vegetation including mangroves and lagoons. There are several small, and two large, saline lagoons (Laguna Grande and Laguna de Navío Quebrado), separated from the Caribbean by sand bars. The

latter is near **Camarones** (take a *colectivo* from the roundabout between the water tower and bus station in Riohacha, US$2.50), which is just off the main road. A swift boat ride (US$0.25) takes you to the park entrance. Some 3 km beyond Camarones lies 'La Playa', a popular beach to which some *colectivos* continue at weekends. The two large lagoons are fed by several intermittent streams which form deltas at the south point of the lakes and are noted for the many colonies of flamingos, some of which are there all year, others gather between November and May, during the wet season when some fresh water enters the lagoons. The birds are believed to migrate to and from the Dutch Antilles, Venezuela and Florida. There is also plenty of other birdlife throughout the year.

Across **Laguna de Navío Quebrado** is a warden's hut on the sand bar, ask to be ferried across by local fishermen or the park guards who are very helpful. There is a visitor centre and some basic and rather pricey accommodation, *cabañas* (**$$-$**) and hammocks (**$**). Beware that it gets very windy and sleeping in hammocks can be uncomfortable.

Riohacha

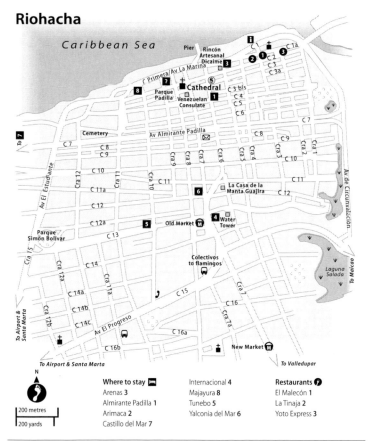

Where to stay 🛏
Arenas **3**
Almirante Padilla **1**
Arimaca **2**
Castillo del Mar **7**

Internacional **4**
Majayura **8**
Tunebo **5**
Yalconia del Mar **6**

Restaurants 🍴
El Malecón **1**
La Tinaja **2**
Yoto Express **3**

Música tropical

No country in South America has a greater variety of musical genres than Colombia, and nowhere is music more abundant than in the fertile breeding grounds of the North Coast. The diversity of musical expression comes from a mixture of African, indigenous and European influences.

On the coast, *música tropical* is an umbrella term used to encompass the many hybrids that have arisen over the years. Most popular among these is *vallenato*, a form of music which originated with farmers around Valledupar and which primarily uses the accordion, *guacharaca* (a tube, made from the trunk of a small palm tree, with ridges carved into it, which when scraped with a fork produces a beat) and the *caja vallenata* (a cylindrical drum brought over by African slaves) as its instruments.

Vallenato is the current favourite but it has its roots in a more ancient genre,

cumbia. *Cumbia* began as a courtship dance practiced among the slave population – it is believed to derive from Guinean *cumbe* – and later mixed with European and indigenous instruments, such as the guitar, the accordion and the *gaita*, a type of flute used by the *indígenas* of the Sierra Nevada de Santa Marta. *Cumbia* is celebrated for bringing together Colombia's three main ethnic groups and it was used as an expression of resistance during the campaign for Independence from the Spanish. *Cumbia* has many other derivatives, such as *porro*, *gaita*, *fandango* and *bullerengue*.

The newest genre to emerge is *champeta*. This is the most African of the genres, it takes its influence from *soukous* and *compas*, and is characterized by very sensual dancing. It gained popularity among the black population of Cartagena and San Basilio de Palenque in the 1980s.

Camping is permitted near the centre. Take plenty of water if walking. The locals survive, after the failure of the crustaceans in the lagoons, on tourism and ocean fishing. There are several bars/restaurants and two shops on the beach, but food is expensive.

Valledupar → *For listings, see pages 78-81. Phone code: 5. Population 354,000.*

South of Riohacha on an alternative road to Maicao and the Venezuelan border is **Cuestecita (Hotel Turismo)**, where you can turn southwest to **Barrancas**, with one of the largest coal mines in the world, **El Cerrejón** ① *T595 5554, cerrejonvisitas@cerrejon.com, for information about pre-arranged visits to the mine.* Continuing on this road, which takes you either round the Sierra Nevada to Barranquilla and Santa Marta via Fundación (see above) or south to Bucaramanga, you come to **Valledupar**, capital of César Department.

The Alfonso López Pumarejo **airport** is on the southern outskirts of the city, 3 km from the centre, and a short walk from the bus terminal. A taxi to the centre will cost US$3. The **bus terminal** ① *Av Salguero (Cra 7A) No 44-156*, is 3 km down the road to Robles and Maicao.

One of the few old buildings in the town, which was founded in the middle of the 16th century, is the **Iglesia La Concepción** which overlooks the central plaza named after a past president, Alfonso López Pumarejo. Nearby is a fine balconied colonial façade of the **Casa del Maestre Pavejeau**, and there is an interesting display of indigenous cultures in the **Casa de la Cultura** ① *Cra 6, No 16A-24, T572 3271*. Valledupar claims to be the home of the *vallenato* music. Each April (26-30), *El Festival de la Leyenda Vallenata* draws thousands of visitors. There are *casas de cambio* on Calle 16. There's a **tourist office** ① *in Gobernación, Cra 12, No 16-120, T574 8230*.

Guajira Peninsula → *For listings, see pages 78-81.*

Beyond Riohacha to the east is the arid and sparsely inhabited Guajira Peninsula, with its magnificent sunsets. The indigenous peoples here, the Wayúu, collect *dividivi* (pods from a strangely wind-bent tree, the *Caesalpina coriaria*, which are mainly used for tanning), tend goats and fish. Increasingly, thanks to government schemes, they are also involved in tourism. Look out for the coloured robes worn by the women.

Arriving in the Guajira Peninsula
To visit the peninsula you can book a tour with one of the many tour companies in Riohacha (see What to do, page 80). Alternatively, you can catch a ride in a *carrito*, a taxi shared with three others, on the paved road to Uribia or Manaure (one hour 30 minutes, US$7) and from there on dirt tracks to Cabo de la Vela (two to three hours).

Manaure and around
Manaure is known for its salt flats southwest of the town. Hundreds of workers dig the salt and collect it in wheelbarrows, a bizarre sight against the glaring white background. If you walk along the beach for an hour, past the salt works, there are several lagoons where flamingos gather. Around 14 km from Manaure in this direction is **Musichi**, an important haunt of the flamingo, sometimes out of the wet season. Note that they may be on the other side of the lagoon and difficult to see. You can hire a moto-taxi in Manaure that will take you towards Musichi to see the flamingos.

From Manaure there are early morning busetas to **Uribia** (30 minutes, US$1-2), and from there to Maicao, another hour. In Uribia, known as the indigenous capital of Colombia, you can buy authentic local handicrafts by asking around, but the town really doesn't have much to its name. It's also full of Venezuelan contraband and has a rough and ready feel to it. There is a **Wayúu festival** here annually in May, and *alijunas* (white people) are welcome, but ask permission before taking photographs. You can get *camionetas* from Uribia to **Cabo de la Vela** (about three hours once everyone has been dropped off at their various *rancherías*, US$5-7.50; *busetas* run until 1400, few on Sunday, all transport leaves from the market). The drive is spectacular with the final few kilometres involving a bumpy ride across a shimmering, dried-out salt lake that generates mirages. Cabo de la Vela is where the Wayúu believe their souls go after death, and is known as Jepirra. In recent years tourism has really taken off and there are now more hostels in Cabo de la Vela than in Riohacha itself, all of them following the two-mile bay. The barren landscape of shrubs and cacti only serves to accentuate the colour of the water, which glimmers in a dozen shades of aquamarine. There are various excursions from Cabo de la Vela, to Pilón de Azúcar mountain, with lovely views of the sea, nearby beach and also a lighthouse, on a different bay. The beach is beautiful and don't forget to look up at night for spectacular starry skies.

Getting to Cabo de la Vela independently is a time-consuming and at times uncomfortable experience, particularly during or immediately after, the wet season, although it can be done. It is far easier (but more expensive) to book a tour from Riohacha.

Macuira National Park

ⓘ *Free entry. Registration and 30-min compulsory induction at Nazareth park office, guides US$20.*

Towards the northeast tip of the Guajira Peninsula is the Serranía de Macuira, named after the Makui people, ancestors of the Wayúu. The 25,000-ha park is entirely within the Wayúu reservation. It consists of a range of hills over 500 m, with microclimates of their own creating an oasis of tropical forest in the semi-desert. The highest point is **Cerro Palúa**, 865 m, and two other peaks are over 750 m. Moisture comes mainly from the northeast, which forms clouds in the evening that disperse in the early morning. The average temperature is 29°C and there is 450 mm of mist/rain providing water for the streams that disappear into the sand once they reach the plains. Macuira's remoteness gives it interesting flora and fauna and notable wildlife includes the cardinal bird and 15 species of snake, including coral snakes. There are also Wayúu settlements little affected by outsiders, where the indigenous people cultivate cashew nuts, coconuts and plantains, as well as collecting dividivi pods. The rangers are all locals and are very friendly. A recommended walk in the park is a visit to the 40-m-high **El Chorro** waterfall, a delightful lush, green area.

Beyond Macuira is **Punta Gallinas**, the northernmost point in South America and a spectacular location. Nearby is **Taroa**, where sand dunes drop directly into the sea – perfect for a swim, but beware the waves are powerful here and the currents can be strong. Spending a few days exploring this area is a remarkable and rewarding experience. The landscape, usually arid and desolate, turns a bright shade of green after the rainy season and there are gorgeous bays for swimming and chilling. It's also the perfect place for getting closer to Wayúu culture and traditions.

Arriving in Macuira National Park To reach the Parque Natural Nacional Macuira you must travel northeast from Uribia along the mineral railway, then either round the coast past Bahía Portete, or direct across the semi-desert, to Nazareth on the east side of the park. There are no tourist facilities anywhere nearby and no public transport, though trucks may take you from the Bahía Portete area to **Nazareth** (six to eight hours), if you can find one. Nazareth is a Wayúu village where you can stay the night. Food and local guides are available. The best way to visit is to contract your own jeep and guide; **Kaí Eco Travel** ⓘ *T717 7173, www.kaieco travel.com*, run by a network of indigenous families, is recommended. A full tour of the peninsula, with visits to Cabo de la Vela, Parque Natural Nacional Macuira and Punta Gallinas costs US$540 per person for 8 days, including transport, accommodation and food, US$350 not including the national park or US$95 for two days. Beyond Cabo de la Vela we strongly advise you take a tour (see page 80) as there is no public transport, little Spanish is spoken and the locals aren't always welcoming. This is also a semi-self governing zone, replete with Venezuelan contraband. **Eco-Guías** in Bogotá and **Aventure Colombia** in Cartagena also arrange trips here from time to time.

Note The Guajira Peninsula is not a place to travel alone, parties of three or more are recommended. If going in your own transport, check the situation before setting out. The roads can be in very bad condition, mostly dirt tracks and these can become impassable around the wet season. When the road is bad Punta Gallinas is only reached by boat from near Cabo de la Vela, two to three hours, often choppy and very wet. Also remember it is hot, it is easy to get lost, there is little mobile cover and very little water. Locals, including police, are very helpful in giving lifts.

Maicao → *Phone code: 5. Population: 103,000.*
The paved Caribbean coastal highway, continues from Riohacha inland to Maicao, 78 km, close to the Venezuelan border. Now that there are no flights from Barranquilla to Maracaibo, taxi or bus to Maicao and *colectivo* to Maracaibo is the most practical route. There is a new bus terminal to the east of town.

Maicao is full of Venezuelan contraband, and is still at the centre of the drugs trade. It has a real Wild West feel to it. Most commercial premises close before 1500, and after 1600 the streets are unsafe, though in recent years security has improved somewhat.

◉ East to Venezuela listings → *Phone code: 5.*

For sleeping and eating price codes and other relevant information, see pages 8-13.

🛏 Where to stay

Riohacha *p75, map p74*
$$$ Arimaca, C 1, No 8-75, T727 3481, www.hotelarimaca.com. Impressive high tower with clean, light and spacious rooms, some with reception room, all with balconies and magnificent sea views. There is a fine swimming pool on 2nd floor, a good restaurant and buffet breakfast is included.
$$$ Hotel Majayura, Cra 10 1-40, T728 8666, majayurasol@hotmail.com. New hotel centrally located near the beach. Restaurant, Internet access, a/c, minibar and buffet breakfast included.
$$ Hotel Arenas, Cra 5, No 1-25, T727 5424, www.guajirahotelarenas.com. Clean rooms if a little dark, with cable TV and a/c. Helpful staff and near the beach.
$ Almirante Padilla, Cra 6/C 3a, T727 2328. Crumbling but with character, has an inviting patio and a restaurant with cheap *almuerzo*. It's clean, friendly, large and very central. Some rooms with a/c.

$ Castillo del Mar, C 9A 15-352, T727 5043, www.hotelcastillodelmariohacha.com. Pleasant hotel by the sea, a bit rough around the edges, but very reasonably priced. Large rooms with a/c or fan. Recommended.
$ Internacional, Cra 7, No 13-37, T727 3483. Down an alleyway off the old market, friendly with a pleasant restaurant on the patio. Free iced water. Recommended.
$ Tunebo, Cra 10, No 12A-02, T728 8174, marytunebo@hotmail.com. A few blocks from the action, but very friendly staff. Near the old market. Also organizes tours. Recommended.
$ Yalconia del Mar, Cra 7, No 11-26, T727 3487. Private bath, clean, safe, friendly, helpful, halfway between beach and bus station.

Valledupar *p75*
$$ Vajamar, Cra 7, No 16A-30, T574 3939, www.hotelvajamar.com. With breakfast, pool and expensive food.
$ Hotel/Restaurant Nutibara, C19, No 9-19, T574 3225. Rooms with a/c, breakfast included.

$ Provincia Hostel, C 16A No 5-25, T580 0558, www.provinciavalledupar.com. New hostel with both dorms and private rooms. There are plenty of chilling spots including hammocks, patio and common rooms. BBQ area, free bikes to borrow and eco-tours of the area.

$ Residencia El Triunfo, C 19, No 9-31. Small rooms with fan, clean and with bath.

Manaure and around p76

Manaure
$ Palaaima, Cr 6, No 7-25, T717 8195. Comfortable, cool rooms with a/c or fan, helpful. There are always Wayúu locals hanging around the hotel who are eager to talk about their culture and traditions.

Uribia
There are cheaper somewhat gotty options.
$ Hotel Juyasirain, C 14A 9-06, T717 7284. The only slightly more upmarket hotel in Uribia. Large, light and airy with a patio restaurant.

Cabo de la Vela
Along the coast, ask anyone and you will probably be able to get fried fish, coconut rice and a place to sling a hammock (US$7). There are now some 60 hostels along the beach, all offering roughly the same set-up for the same cost. Try **Playa Bonita**, in the main cluster of houses and shops, or **Pujurú**, further up the beach towards Pilón de Azúcar.

Punta Gallinas
$ Luz Mila. A lonely, but friendly little hostel and restaurant run by the Wayúu and where **Kai Eco Travel** (see below) has a base for their tours. Recommended.

Maicao p78
$$ Hotel Maicao Internacional, C 12, No 10-90, T726 7184. Good rooms with a/c, friendly staff and a rooftop swimming pool and bar. A good option in Maicao.

$$ Los Medanos, Cra 10, No 11-25, T726 8822. This hotel has clean, large rooms, though they are a bit dark. Extras include a/c, cable TV, minibar, a restaurant and a disco. Its private bathrooms have cold water only.

$$ Maicao Plaza, C 10, No 10-28, T726 6597. Clean and spacious, this hotel offers a/c, cable TV, and en suite bathrooms with cold water.

$ El Dorado, Cra 10, No 12-45, T726 7242. A little dilapidated, but it has a/c, TV and a good water supply.

🍴 Restaurants

Riohacha p75, map p74
Many ice cream and juice bars, and small *asados*, serving large, cheap selections of barbecued meat can be found at the western end of the seafront and there is also a row of picturesque, brightly painted huts serving ceviche and fresh seafood. The eastern end has more restaurants for sit-down meals.

$$ El Malecón, C 1, No 3-43. Good selection of seafood and meats served in a palm-thatched barn looking out to sea. There is music and dancing in the evenings. A good place for people-watching.

$$ La Tinaja, C 1, 4-59. Excellent seafood in light, breezy restaurant. Try the *Delicias de la casa* rice dish, tasty and substantial. Recommended.

$ Yoto Express, C 1, 3-42. Economic restaurant serving sandwiches and some Mexican specialities.

Manaure and around p76

Cabo de la Vela
$$-$ El Caracol. Expensive but good, serving catch of the day (try the *langostina al ajillo*).

Valledupar p75
$ Hotel/Restaurant Nutibara, next door to **Residencia El Triunfo**. Cheap meals, excellent fruit juices.

Hammocks

There's no better way to enjoy Colombia's beaches than to relax in a hammock, and there are abundant conveniently located palm trees to use as supports. Plenty of places hire them out but for true comfort it's best to buy your own.

The hammocks developed by the Wayúu are made up of intricately woven threads of cotton that form a crocheted net. These are known as *chinchorros* and they are larger than the average hammock, with wrap-around sides serving as a blanket and they often feature elaborate tassels. The other most common style uses brightly coloured woven cotton or wool to form a large stretch of material.

San Jacinto, a couple of hours south of Cartagena, is the capital of Colombia's hammock industry and the best place to find a bargain, but the market in Santa Marta also has a good selection. For *chinchorros*, the best places are the market in Riohacha and Uribia's handicraft shops in La Guajira.

☺ Festivals

Riohacha *p75, map p74*
Mar Festival Francisco el Hombre.
Vallenato festival.

Valledupar *p75*
Apr Festival de la Leyenda Vallenata, www.festivalvallenato.com. One of the most important music festivals in Colombia.

○ Shopping

Riohacha *p75, map p74*
Good hammocks sold in the market. The best place for buying local items is **La Casa de la Manta Guajira**, Cra 6/C 12. Be prepared to bargain.

▲ What to do

Riohacha *p75, map p74*

Tour operators
Guajira Viva, C 3, No 5-08, loc 1, T727 0607. 5-day tours to Alta Guajira, Cabo de la Vela, Santuario de Fauna y Flora los Flamencos.
Lucho Freyle, T728 2885, T312-647 1434 (mob). Wayúu guide in Riohacha, jeep tours around La Guajira and Cabo de la Vela.

Operadora Turística Wayúu, C 1A, No 4-35, T311-400 7985 (mob). Wayúu-run and can be found on the seafront. Sells beautiful, colourful Wayúu *mochilas*. Organizes tours to *rancherías* and Cabo de la Vela.
Kaí Eco Travel, based at Hotel Castillo del Mar, C 9A 15-352, T717 7173, T311-436 2830 (mob), www.kaiecotravel.com. Run by a network of Wayúu families, organizes tours to Cabo de la Vela, Parque Natural Nacional Macuira, Punta Gallinas, the northernmost point of South America, costs from US$95 for 2 days, to US$540 for 8 days per person, including transport, accommodation and food. Highly recommended.

Uribia
Kaishi, T311-429 6315, T316-429 6315 (mob). Speak to Andrés Orozco, this company organizes jeep tours around La Guajira.

◉ Transport

Riohacha *p75, map p74*
Early morning is best for travel, transport is scarce in the afternoon.

Air
1 flight a day **Bogotá**, Avianca; where connections to other cities can be made. Flights to **Aruba** Tue and Sat.

Bus

It is best to travel from Riohacha in a luxury bus, in the early morning, as these are less likely to be stopped and searched for contraband. **Brasilia** runs Pullman buses to **Maicao**, every 30 mins from 0630-1700, US$5.50.

Brasilia also has buses to **Santa Marta** ($US8.50, 3 hrs) and **Cartagena** every 30 mins. No direct buses to **Cabo de la Vela**: travel to **Uribia** and wait for a jeep (leaves when full). It's a long and uncomfortable journey. Some *colectivos* for Uribia and the northeast leave from the new market, 2 km southeast on the Valledupar road.

Taxi

Coopcaribe Taxis travel throughout the region and can be picked up almost anywhere in town, especially close to the old market area near the Hotel Internacional or outside Drogas La Rebaja. Daily to **Uribia**, 1½ hrs, US$7; **Manaure**, 1¾ hrs, US$8. They leave when full (4 people), be prepared to pay slightly more if there are no travellers.

Colectivos for the Flamingo Sanctuary leave from the large roundabout between the market and bus station, US$2.50.

Valledupar *p75*

Air

There are flights to **Bogotá** and **Barranquilla** with **Aires**.

Bus

To **Barranquilla**, 5-6 hrs, US$12.50; **Bucaramanga**, 8 hrs US$30, 7 a day with Copetran; **Santa Marta**, 4½ hrs, US$11; **Cartagena**, US$13 with **Expreso Brasilia**, US$20, 6 a day with Copetran.

Maicao *p78*

Bus

Brasilia has a service every 30 mins from 0630-1700 to **Riohacha**, US$5.50, **Copetrán** has 3 a day, US$5; **Santa Marta**, 3 hrs, US$12.50; **Barranquilla**, 4-5 hrs, US$15; **Cartagena**, 6 hrs, US$20.

2 daily to **Bogotá** at 0930 and 1430 with Copetran, US$50; to **Medellín**, 3 daily, 0915, 1330, 1615, US$77. Regular service to **Barranquilla**, US$15-22.

● Directory

Riohacha *p75, map p74*
Banks Most are on Parque Almirante. **Banco de Colombia**, Cra 7, between C 2/3, for Visa, Mon-Fri, 0800-1800, Sat, 0900-1200. **Banco de Bogotá**, Cra 9/C 3, Mon-Fri 0800-1200 and 1400-1600 **Embassies and consulates** Venezuela, Cra 7, No 3-08, p7-B, T727 4076, F727 3967, Mon-Thu 0900-1300, Fri 0900-1500, if you need a visa, you should check all requirements for your nationality before arriving at this consulate. Travellers report it is easier to get a Venezuelan visa in Barranquilla. **Immigration** DAS Office (immigration) C 5 y Cra 5, open 0800-1200, 1400-1800. **Internet and telephone** On Parque Almirante. **Post** C 2, Cra 6/7.

Valledupar *p75*
Banks You can change money at *casas de cambio* on Calle 16.

San Andrés and Providencia

San Andrés and Providencia are destinations most Colombians dream about visiting at least once in their lifetime. Closer to Nicaragua than to the Colombian mainland – there is a running dispute between the two countries over sovereignty – these Caribbean islands have what locals have dubbed 'the sea of seven colours', though it often seems like more. The waters around this archipelago play host to a variety of marine life, and the clarity of the sea makes this one of the best diving destinations in the Caribbean. In 2000, UNESCO declared the archipelago a World Biosphere Reserve, christened **The Seaflower**. At 32 km in length, the Old McBean Lagoon barrier reef off Providencia is the third largest in the world.

Background
San Andrés and Providencia share a coastline rich in coral reefs, white-sand cays and waters of extraordinary colours, but are in fact very different. San Andrés, the larger island, is a popular mass tourism destination, replete with resort hotels and discos. Providencia has quietly observed its big sister's development, decided it does not want to follow the same path, and has put in place certain restrictions to halt the encroachment of package tourism.

The original inhabitants are mostly the descendants of Jamaican slaves brought over by English pirates such as Henry Morgan, and with the arrival of English, Dutch, French and Spanish settlers over the years this has led to an extraordinary genealogical mix. Today, especially in San Andrés, much of the original culture has been diluted and about 50% of the population is now made up of immigrants from mainland Colombia. The remainder are locals and there are Lebanese and Turkish communities too. Immigration is less pronounced in Providencia.

San Andrés and Providencia are famous in Colombia for their different styles of music, including the local form of calypso, soca, reggae and church music, as well as schottische, quadrille, polka and mazurka, the musical legacies of the various European communities that settled here. A number of good local groups perform on the islands and in Colombia. Concerts are held at the **Old Coliseum** every Saturday at 2100 in the high season. There is a cultural centre at Punta Hansa in San Andrés town.

After Colombus spotted the islands on his fourth trip to the Caribbean, their early colonial history was dominated by the conflicts between Spain and England, though the Dutch occupied Providencia for some years. English Puritans arrived on Providencia from Bermuda and England in 1629 and later moved to San Andrés. The English left in 1641, but Creole English remained the dominant language until recent times and is still widely spoken. Surnames such as Whittaker, Hooker, Archbold, Robinson, Howard and Newell are also common. Providencia later became a pirate colony, shared between the Dutch and the English before it was taken back by the Spanish and assigned to the Vice Royalty of New Granada (modern-day Colombia) in 1803. In 1818 French Corsair Louis-Michel Aury successfully invaded Providencia and declared it part of the United States of Argentina and Chile, using it to capture Spanish cargo to bolster the burgeoning Latin American Independence movement. Finally, in 1822 San Andrés, Providencia and Santa Catalina were incorporated into the newly independent state of Gran Colombia.

The islands are 770 km north of continental Colombia, 849 km southwest of Jamaica, and 240 km east of Nicaragua. This proximity has led Nicaragua to claim them from

Colombia in the past. Three battleships patrol San Andrés to guard against any invasion by the Nicaraguans.

San Andrés and around → *For listings, see pages 88-91. Phone code: 8. Population: 77,000.*

San Andrés, a coral island, is 11 km long, rising at its highest to 120 m. The town, commercial centre, major hotel sector and airport are at the northern end. A good view of the town can be seen from **El Cliff**. San Andrés is a popular, safe and local holiday destination for Colombians.

Arriving in San Andrés

Getting there A cheap way to visit San Andrés is by taking a charter flight from Bogotá or another major city for a weekend or a week, with accommodation and food included. See the newspapers, which usually have supplements on Wednesday or Thursday. Standards of hotel and restaurant packages can vary greatly. You may wish to go for a cheap airfare and choose where to stay on arrival. The airport is 15 minutes' walk from town. Buses to the centre and San Luis go from across the road. A taxi is US$5.50, a *colectivo* US$0.70. Cruise ships and tours go to San Andrés but there are no other official passenger services by sea. ▸▸ *See Transport, page 91.*

Getting around Buses run every 15 minutes on the eastern side of the island, US$0.30, and more often at night and during the holidays. Taxis around the island cost US$11, but in town fares double after 2200.

Bicycles are easy to hire but are usually in poor condition, so choose your own bike and check all parts thoroughly. Motorbikes and golf buggies are also easy to hire.

Tourist information Staff at the **tourist office** ① *at the airport, Circunvalar Av Newball, Edif Coral Palace, www.sanandres. gov.co/turismo, Mon-Fri 0800-1200, 1400-1800*, are helpful and English is spoken. They can also provide maps and hotel lists. On arrival in San Andrés, you must buy a tourist card, US$9, which is also valid for Providencia so don't lose it. You must also have an onward or return ticket.

① **San Andrés Island**

Punta Norte
Johnny Cay
Bahía Sardinas
Punta Hansa
San Andrés
Punta Paraíso
Roca del Pescador
1
Bahía de San Andrés
Caribbean Sea
Baptist Church
Bahía Baja
La Loma (104m)   2
Seaquarium
El Acuario
La Laguna
① Haynes Cay
Cueva de Morgan
Rocky Cay
N
San Luis
El Cove
Bahía Sonora
1 km
1 miles
Monte Derecho
Where to stay
Casa Harb 1
Sunset 3
La Piscinita
Súper Decameron Marazul 2
3
Restaurants
Bibi's Place 1
Hoyo Soplador
➡ **San Andrés maps**
Punta Sur
1 San Andrés island, page 83
2 San Andrés town, page 84

Places on San Andrés

Besides the beautiful cays and beaches on the eastern side, see **Hoyo Soplador** (South End), a geyser-like hole through which the sea spouts into the air when the wind is in the right direction. The west coast is less spoilt, but there are no beaches on this side. Instead there is **El Cove** (The Cove), the island's deepest anchorage, and **Cueva de Morgan** (Morgan's Cave), reputed hiding place for pirate's treasure, which is penetrated by the sea through an underwater passage. Next to Cueva de Morgan is a **pirate museum** ① *entry US$1*, with exhibitions telling the history of the coconut, lots of paraphernalia salvaged from wrecks around the island and a replica pirate ship. The museum is run by Jimmy Gordon, author of *Legado de Piratas*, who has extensive knowledge of the island's history. About 1 km south from Cueva de Morgan is **West View** ① *daily 0900-1700, entry US$1.10 including bread to feed the fish*, an excellent place to see marine life as the sea is very clear. There is a small jetty with a diving board and slide, and you can hire Aqua Nauta equipment (US$50 for 30 minutes), old-fashioned diving equipment with oxygen piped through a tube to a helmet. There is a small restaurant opposite the entrance.

At El Cove, you can continue round the coast, or cross the centre of the island back to town over **La Loma**. This is the highest point on the island and nearby is **La Laguna**, a freshwater lake 30 m deep, home to many birds and surrounded by palm and mango trees. On the town side of La Loma is the first **Baptist Church** to be built on the island (1847), acting as a beacon to shipping. The church has a Sunday service from 1000-1300 with gospel singing. If you take a turning just before the church you will reach the **Mirador Escalona**, a lookout point on someone's unfinished roof (US$1), from which there are spectacular views of the island. In the centre of the island you will find some life as it was before San Andrés became a tourist destination, with clapboard houses and traditional music.

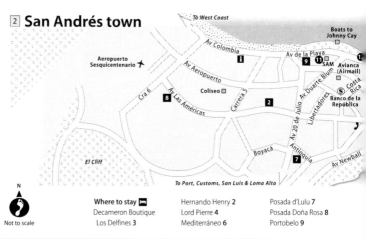

2 San Andrés town

To West Coast

Boats to Johnny Cay

Aeropuerto Sesquicentenario ✈

Av Colombia
Av de la Playa
Av Aeropuerto
Cra 6
Av Las Américas
Coliseo
Carrera 5
Av Duarte Blum
Av 20 de Julio
Libertadores
SAM
Avianca (Airmail)
Costa Rica
Banco de la República
El Cliff
Boyacá
Antioquia
Av Newball

To Port, Customs, San Luis & Loma Alta

N
Not to scale

Where to stay 🛏
Decameron Boutique
Los Delfines **3**
Hernando Henry **2**
Lord Pierre **4**
Mediterráneo **6**
Posada d'Lulu **7**
Posada Doña Rosa **8**
Portobelo **9**

Around San Andrés

Boats leave from San Andrés in the morning for El Acuario and Haynes Cay, and continue to Johnny Cay (frequently spelt Jhonny) in the afternoon, which has a white beach and parties all day Sunday (US$16.60 return). **El Acuario** has crystalline water and is a good place to snorkel, and see eagle and manta rays. You can wade across the water to **Haynes Cay** where there is good food and a reggae bar at Bibi's Place. These are popular tours; if you want to avoid the crowds a good option is to hire a private boat (US$110 for the day) and do the tour in reverse. Boats for the cays leave from Tonino's Marina between 0930 and 1030, returning at 1530, or from Muelle Casa de la Cultura on Avenida Newell.

Apart from those already mentioned, other cays and islets in the archipelago are **Bolívar**, **Albuquerque**, **Algodón** (included in the Sunrise Park development in San Andrés), **Rocky**, the **Grunt**, **Serrana**, **Serranilla** and **Quitasueño**. On San Andrés the beaches are in town and on the eastern coast. Perhaps the best is at **San Luis** and **Bahía Sonora** (Sound Bay).

Diving

Diving off San Andrés is very good; the depth varies from 3-30 m, visibility from 30-60 m. There are three types of site: walls of seaweed and minor coral reefs, large groups of different types of coral, and underwater plateaux with much marine life. It is possible to dive in 70% of the insular platform. The **Pared Azul** (**Blue Wall**) is excellent for deep-water diving. **Black Coral Net** and **Morgam's Sponge** are other good sites. ▸▸ *For further information, see What to do, page 90.*

Providencia → *For listings, see pages 88-91. Phone code: 8.*

Providencia, also called **Old Providence**, 80 km to the north-northeast of San Andrés, is 7 km long and 3.5 km wide. The island is more mountainous and considerably more verdant than San Andrés, rising to 360 m, due to its volcanic origin and is much older. There are waterfalls, and the land drops steeply into the sea in places.

Providencia is striving to retain its cultural identity. Hotels must be constructed in the typical clapboard style of the island and cannot be built higher than two storeys, while mainland operators cannot manage them directly; they must work in partnership with local owners. Only locals are allowed to buy property on the island and outsiders can stay no longer than six months at a time.

Arriving on Providencia

Getting there Visitors can arrive by air from San Andrés (20 minutes) or by sea on launches and boats that ferry goods over to Providencia. Beware that the sea can be choppy on this trip.

> ➡ **San Andrés maps**
> 1 San Andrés island, page 83
> 2 San Andrés town, page 84

Restaurants 🍴
Guillos Café **11**
La Fonda Antioqueña **12**
Margherita e Carbonara **13**
Niko's **14**

Getting around *Chivas* (brightly coloured buses) circle the island at more or less regular intervals, the standard fare is US$1.60. *Colectivos* can also be found on the island and charge much the same.

Tourist office In Palacio de la Alcaldía, T514 8054, alcalde@providencia.gov.co.

Around the island

Day tours are arranged through hotels around the island, stopping typically at Cayo Cangrejo to swim and snorkel, they cost about US$17. Snorkelling equipment can be hired and diving trips arranged: the best places are Aguadulce and South West Bay.

In 1996 part of the east coast and offshore reefs and coral islands were declared a National Park (**Parque Nacional Natural Old Providence – McBean Lagoon**). The land

Providencia

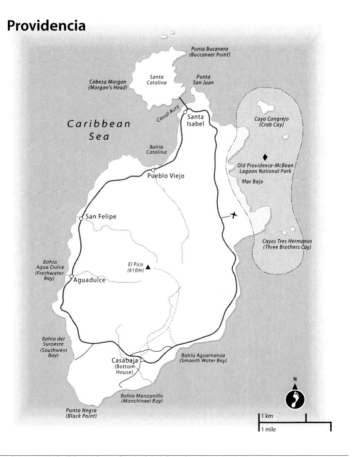

The black crabs of Providencia

With the arrival of the first rains between April and June, Providencia is the scene a spectacular natural phenomenon. Each night during the wet season thousands of black crabs (*Gecarcinus lateralis*) descend from the forests of High Hill and release their eggs in the waters between South West Bay and Freshwater, wriggling their abdomens in the surf to deposit their eggs. The hatchlings are born in the sea and return to the hills one month later.

During the migration the road that encircles the island is closed to traffic, thus allowing the crabs free access to the beaches without the risk of being run over. Coralina, the government's environmental agency on the archipelago, has banned the capture and eating of crabs during the breeding season and anyone caught disobeying the ban risks a heavy fine equivalent to three months of the minimum wage.

Many of the islanders make a living from crab fishing but during this time hunters turn protectors as they are employed as enforcers of the ban, thus ensuring that Providencia's black crab population will continue to thrive.

position includes Iron Wood Hill (150 m), mainly small trees but including cockspur (*Acacia colinsii*) which has large conical-shaped needles, home to a species of ant (*Pseudo-myrmex ferruginea*) with a very painful sting. There are superb views from **Casabaja** (Bottom House) or **Aguamansa** (Smooth Water), a climb to the summit will take about one hour, and with a guide will cost US$13.80. You will see relics of the fortifications built on the island during its disputed ownership.

Horse riding is available, and boat trips can be made to neighbouring islands such as **Santa Catalina**, an old pirate lair separated from Providencia by a channel cut for their better defence. To the northeast is **Cayo Cangrejo** (Crab Cay), a beautiful place for swimming and snorkelling, and **Cayos Tres Hermanos** (Three Brothers Cays). Boat trips leave from 1000-1500 and cost about US$17 per person, with a two hour lunch in South West Bay. Santa Catalina is joined to the main island by a 100-m wooden bridge, known as the **Puente de los Amantes** (Lovers' Bridge). On the west side of Santa Catalina are the ruins of an old fort, built by the English to defend their pirate colony. Formerly known as Fort Warwick, it was rechristened **Fuerte de la Libertad** after the island was taken back by the Spanish in the 17th century. The fort still has the original canons and it is rumoured that there is a secret cave which was used by Henry Morgan to escape to the sea below (most probably untrue). Beyond the fort is a fine beach, excellent for snorkelling, with caves with air chambers and lots of starfish. Further still is a rock formation called **Morgan's Head**; seen from the side it looks like a man's profile. The path beyond Morgan's Head leads through thick forest to the top of the mountain and an abandoned house formerly belonging to a drug trafficker.

The beaches

Bahía Manzanillo (Manchineel Bay) is named after the manzanillo trees found on its edges (the fruit is like a miniature apple, sweet smelling but with an acid taste – and dangerous; do not eat), and is the largest, most attractive and least developed, with a couple of restaurants, including **Roland's Reggae bar** (see page 90). **Bahía del Suroeste** (South West Bay) is fringed by almond trees, palms and has bottle green water, and on Saturday afternoons the local boys put on bareback horse races. **Bahía Agua Dulce** (Freshwater Bay) has a small strip of beach and the sea laps at the fronts of the many hotels in this small bay. Two smaller beaches are **Alan's Bay**, between Aguadulce and San Felipe, which is very secluded and seldom visited, and **Playa del Fuerte**, underneath the fort on Santa Catalina, which has excellent snorkelling and lots of starfish.

◉ San Andrés and Providencia listings → *Phone code: 8.*

For sleeping and eating price codes and other relevant information, see pages 8-13.

◎ Where to stay

San Andrés *p83, maps p83 and p84*

$$$$ Casa Harb, C 11, No 10-83, La Rocosa, T512 6348, www.casaharb.com. Just outside town, this boutique hotel takes its inspiration from the Far East and is the most stylish location on the island. Each room is individually decorated with antique furniture. The baths, made of solid granite, are enormous. A former family home, this mansion has a an infinity pool and offers home-cooked meals.

$$$$ Hotel Súper Decameron Marazul, Km 4 Vía San Luis, T513 2600, www.decameron. com. This enormous all-inclusive resort hotel sits on the southern end of town on the way to San Luis. It has a private beach, pool, 3 restaurants and a disco.

$$$$ Lord Pierre, Av Colombia, No 1B-106, T512 7541, www.lordpierre.com. While it may boast a magnificent pier on the tip of the *malecón*, this hotel needs a rehaul. Rooms are large but a little dated, with heavy furniture.

$$$ Decameron Boutique Los Delfines, Av Colombia, No 1B-86, T512 7816, www.decameron.com. Another hotel in the **Decameron** chain, this one achieves some individuality. The rooms are particularly comfortable, all painted a cool white and set around a fine pool. There is also a restaurant on a jetty, under which large schools of fish congregate for feeding.

$$$ Portobelo, Av Colombia, No 5A-69, T512 7008, www.portobelohotel.com.

Occupies a couple of buildings on western end of the *malecón*. Rooms have large beds, a/c and cable TV. Breakfast included.

$$$ Sunset Hotel, Carretera Circunvalar Km 13, T513 0433, sunsetsai@hotmail.com. On the western side of the island, this is the perfect place to stay if you want to do some serious diving – or just want to escape the crowds. It has bright, fresh rooms with high ceilings, all set around a saltwater swimming pool. With a restaurant serving a mixture of international and regional food in a typical clapboard house and a dive shop next door, this is one of the best places to unwind in San Andrés.

$$ Hernando Henry, Av Las Américas, No 4-84, T512 3416. At the back of town, this hotel has shoddy but passable rooms. TV and laundry service. Rooms are significantly cheaper with fan.

$$ La Posada D'Lulú, Av Antioquia, No 2-28, T512 2919, www.descansorural.com. This brightly coloured hostel with its clean and comfortable rooms is one of the best mid-range options in town. There are 2 apartments to rent for longer stays and an excellent restaurant serving home cooked food for US$3. Recommended.

$$ Posada Doña Rosa, Av Las Américas con Aeropuerto, T512 3649, www.posada rosa.blogspot.com. A 2-min walk from the airport, this is a reasonable and economical option. It has clean rooms with private bathrooms and a small patio with potted plants. There is a kitchen and TV room, and it's a short walk from the beach. Also has 2 apartments to rent.

$ Mediterráneo, Av Colón, T512 6722. Noisy, crumbling building near the beach. Rooms just about pass for cleanliness. TV and fridge provided.

Private houses

$ pp Red Crab, Av Circunvalar, San Luis, T513 0314, www.arriendos.biz/RedCrab.html. A villa on the beach with 4 independent apartments, each with a capacity of up to 6 people. Price includes use of a swimming pool and the services of a housekeeper.

Camping

You can camp on Hayes Caye for US$100 pp (includes transport, food and drinks), but you must ask the Port Authority for permission through **Bibi's Place** (see Restaurants, below).

Providencia *p85, map p86*
There are several rooms available for rent at affordable prices in local houses or *posadas nativas*. Try **Captain 'Hippie'**, T514 8548/T311-485 4805 (mob), who offers home-cooked food and lodging in his house (**$** pp).
$$$$ Deep Blue Hotel, Maracaibo Bay, T321-458 2099, www.hoteldeepblue.com. Luxury hotel under new management and recently renovated. **Deep Blue** is set amidst tropical forest and offers splendid views of Crab Caye and the Caribbean. There's a new tapas restaurant by the sea and visitors get complimentary use of the hotel's sea kayaks. Good sustainability and environmental policies. Recommended.
$$$ Cabañas Miss Elma, Aguadulce, T514 8229, philhuffington@yahoo.es. Wood-panelled *cabañas* with terraces, right on the beach. Large rooms, some with reception rooms and baby cots. Cable TV and a/c.
$$$ Hotel Sirius South, South West Bay, T514 8213, www.siriushotel.net. Large, colourful house set back from the beach, run by a Swiss family. The rooms are large and light, some have balconies with hammocks. Kitchen available for guests. Prices negotiable.

$$$ Posada del Mar, Aguadulce, T514 8168, posadadelmar@latinmail.com. Pink and purple clapboard house with comfortable rooms, each with a terrace and hammock looking onto the bay. The sea laps at the edge of the garden. Has cable TV, a/c, minibar and hot water. Recommended.
$$ Cabañas Miss Mary, South West Bay, T514 8206. On the beach at South West Bay, Miss Mary has clean, comfortable rooms with cable TV and hot water. Breakfast is included.
$$ Hotel Old Providence, Santa Isabel, T514 8691. Above supermarket **Erika**, rooms are basic but clean and have a/c, cable TV, fridge and private bathroom.

Camping

Roland's Reggae bar, Playa Manzanillo, T514 8417, rolandsbeach@hotmail.com. Hires tents for camping (**$**).

🍽 Restaurants

San Andrés *p83, maps p83 and p84*
$$ Bibi's Place, Haynes Caye, T513 3767, caritoortega@hotmail.com. Reggae bar and restaurant on cay next to **El Acuario** serving seafood, including crab and lobster. Organizes full moon parties and civil and rasta weddings.
$$ Margherita e Carbonara, Av Colombia, opposite the Lord Pierre Hotel. Italian-owned restaurant decorated with photographs from Italian films. Good pizzas.
$$ Niko's, Av Colombia, No 1-93. Bills itself as a seafood restaurant though its steaks are actually better. Lovely setting by the water.
$ Guillos Café, Av Peatonal next to **Portobelo Hotel**. Fast-food restaurant serving sandwiches and burgers, as well as local specialities.
$ La Fonda Antioqueña, Av La Playa, No 1-16. On the main beach in San Andrés town, this *paisa* restaurant serves good, cheap food.

Providencia *p85, map p86*
Local specialities include crab soup and *rondón*, a mix of fish, conch, yucca and dumplings, cooked in coconut milk. Corn

ice cream is also popular – it tastes a little like vanilla but a little sweeter. Breadfruit, a grapefruit-sized fruit with a taste similar to potato, is the archipelago's official fruit.

$$ Caribbean Place (Donde Martín), Aguadulce. *Bogoteño* chef Martín Quintero arrived for a brief stay in 1989 and has never left. He uses local ingredients. Specialities include lobster in crab sauce, fillet of fish in ginger and corn ice cream.

$$ Roland's Reggae Bar, Playa Manzanillo, T514 8417, rolandsbeach@hotmail.com. Roland is a legend on the island, as are the parties at his bar-restaurant on Manzanillo Beach. The menu is mainly seafood, with fried fish and ceviches.

$ Pizza's Place, Aguadulce. Basic pizzas and pastas.

✪ Festivals

San Andrés *p83, maps p83 and p84*
Jun Jardín del Caribe. A folkloric festival.
20 Jul Independence.
Dec Rainbow Festival. Reggae and calypso.

Providencia *p85, map p86*
Jun Carnival.

▲ What to do

San Andrés *p83, maps p83 and p84*
From Toninos Marina there are boat trips to the nearby cays, US$17 with lunch included.

Canopying
Canopy La Loma, Vía La Loma-Barrack, T314-447 9868 (mob). Has a site at the top of the hill in San Andrés. 3 'flights' over the trees (450 m, 300 m and 200 m above sea level) with spectacular views out to sea, costs US$17. Good safety precautions and equipment.

Diving
Banda Dive Shop, Hotel Lord Pierre, Local 104, T512 2507, www.bandadiveshop.com. PADI qualified, mini-courses from US$83. Fast boat and good equipment.

Sharky Dive Shop, Carretera Circunvalar Km 13, T512 0651, www.sharkydiveshop.com. Next to **Sunset Hotel**, Sharky's has good equipment and excellent, English-speaking guides. PADI qualifications and a beginners' course held in the Sunset s saltwater pool.

Fishing
Cooperativa Lancheros, on the beach in San Andrés town. Can arrange fishing trips. Windsurfing and sunfish sailing rental and lessons are also available from **Bar Boat**, on the road to San Luis (opposite the naval base), 1000-1800 daily (also has floating bar, English and German spoken), and **Windsurf Spot**, Hotel Isleño; waterskiing at **Water Spot**, Hotel Aquarium, and **Jet Sky**.

Watersports and boat trips
Snorkelling equipment can be hired for US$10.
Centro Comercial New Point Plaza, No 234, T512 8787. Morning boats to El Acuario Cay, off Haynes Cay. The trip to watch the colourful fish takes 20 mins and costs US$16 return. They provide mask and sandals as protection against sea-urchins. They also run the *Nautilus*, a glass hull semi-submarine, US$17.
Cooperativa Lancheros, on the beach in San Andrés town. Can arrange windsurfing, jet skiing and kite surfing.

Also try **Windsurf Spot**, Hotel El Isleño, Av Colombia, No 5-117; and **Water Spot**, Decameron Aquarium, Av Colombia, No 1-19, www.decameron.com.

Providencia *p85, map p86*

Diving
Recommended diving spots on the Old McBean Lagoon reef are **Manta's Place**, a good place to see manta rays; **Felipe's Place** where there is a submerged figure of Christ; and **Stairway to Heaven**, which has a large wall of coral and big fish.
Felipe Diving, Cabañas El Ron~ o, Aguadulce, T514 8770, www.felipediving.com. Mini-courses

from US$80, also rents snorkel equipment. Owner Felipe Cabeza even has a diving spot named after him. Warmly recommended.
Sirius Diving, South West Bay, T514 8213, www.siriusdivecenter.com. PADI qualifications, mini-course US$100.

Snorkelling and boat trips
Recommended snorkelling sites include the waters around Santa Catalina, where there are many caves to explore as well as **Morgan's Head** and lots of starfish; **Hippie's Place**, which has a little bit of everything; and **El Faro** (The Lighthouse), the end of the reef before it drops into deep sea, some 14 km from Providencia.
Valentina Tours, T514 8548. Lemus Walter, aka Captain 'Hippie', organizes snorkelling, and boat trips (US$17 per person) to the outlying cays and reefs. He has a section of the reef named after him. He charges US$140 for a day's hire of the boat.

Tour operators
Body Contact, Aguadulce, T514 8283. Owner Jennifer Archbold organizes excursions, fishing and hiking trips, currency exchange, accommodation, and more. Recommended.

Walking
There is a good walk over Manchineel Hill, between Bottom House (Casa Baja) and South West Bay, 1.5 km through tropical forest, with fine views of the sea; many types of bird can seen, along with iguanas and blue lizards. Guided tours depart twice a day at 0900 and 1500 from Bottom House. Enquire at **Body Contact**, see Tour operators, above, or **Coralina**, T514 9003.

⊖ Transport

San Andrés *p83, maps p83 and p84*
Air Flights to **Bogotá**, **Cali**, **Medellín** and **Cartagena** with AeroRepública; Avianca; Satena; and **Searca** (booked through Decameron). **Copa** runs 1 flight daily to **Panama City**. To **Providencia** 2 times a

day with **Satena** and **Searca**. Bookable only in San Andrés.

Boat Cargo ships are not supposed to carry passengers to the mainland, but many do. It's possible to catch a ride on one of the cargo boats to **Providencia** 3 times a week. The journey takes 7-8 hrs and is uncomfortable. Normal price is US$22. They usually leave at 2200, arriving in the early morning. *Miss Isabel*, *Doña Olga* and *Raziman* are 3 boats that make the trip regularly. Speak directly to the captain at the port in San Andrés, or enquire at the Port Authority (*Capitanía del Puerto*) in San Luis. Other offers of tickets on ships from San Andrés, or of a job on a ship, may be a con.The sea crossing to **Cartagena** takes 3-4 days, depending on the weather.

Vehicle and bicycle hire
Motorbikes are easy to hire, as are golf buggies. Cars can be hired for US$22 for 2 hrs, US$65 for a day. Passport may be required as deposit.
Bikes are a popular way of getting around on the island and are easy to hire, eg opposite **Los Delfines Hotel** on Av Colombia, US$2 per hr or US$7 per day.

Providencia *p85, map p86*

Vehicle and bicycle hire
Mopeds can be hired for US$27 per day from many of the hotels (eg **Posada del Mar** in Aguadulce) and golf buggies are also available for US$83 per day.

❻ Directory

San Andrés *p83, maps p83 and p84*
Immigration DAS, right next to airport, T512 7182/T512 5540.

Providencia *p85, map p86*
Emergencies Police: T2. **Medical services**
Ambulance, T514 8016 at hospital;
Medical emergencies, T11.

Contents

Footnotes

Index

Titles available in the Footprint *Focus* range

Latin America	UK RRP	US RRP
Bahia & Salvador	£7.99	$11.95
Buenos Aires & Pampas	£7.99	$11.95
Costa Rica	£8.99	$12.95
Cuzco, La Paz & Lake Titicaca	£8.99	$12.95
El Salvador	£5.99	$8.95
Guadalajara & Pacific Coast	£6.99	$9.95
Guatemala	£8.99	$12.95
Guyana, Guyane & Suriname	£5.99	$8.95
Havana	£6.99	$9.95
Honduras	£7.99	$11.95
Nicaragua	£7.99	$11.95
Paraguay	£5.99	$8.95
Quito & Galápagos Islands	£7.99	$11.95
Recife & Northeast Brazil	£7.99	$11.95
Rio de Janeiro	£8.99	$12.95
São Paulo	£5.99	$8.95
Uruguay	£6.99	$9.95
Venezuela	£8.99	$12.95
Yucatán Peninsula	£6.99	$9.95

Asia	UK RRP	US RRP
Angkor Wat	£5.99	$8.95
Bali & Lombok	£8.99	$12.95
Chennai & Tamil Nadu	£8.99	$12.95
Chiang Mai & Northern Thailand	£7.99	$11.95
Goa	£6.99	$9.95
Hanoi & Northern Vietnam	£8.99	$12.95
Ho Chi Minh City & Mekong Delta	£7.99	$11.95
Java	£7.99	$11.95
Kerala	£7.99	$11.95
Kolkata & West Bengal	£5.99	$8.95
Mumbai & Gujarat	£8.99	$12.95

Africa	UK RRP	US RRP
Beirut	£6.99	$9.95
Damascus	£5.99	$8.95
Durban & KwaZulu Natal	£8.99	$12.95
Fès & Northern Morocco	£8.99	$12.95
Jerusalem	£8.99	$12.95
Johannesburg & Kruger National Park	£7.99	$11.95
Kenya's beaches	£8.99	$12.95
Kilimanjaro & Northern Tanzania	£8.99	$12.95
Zanzibar & Pemba	£7.99	$11.95

Europe	UK RRP	US RRP
Bilbao & Basque Region	£6.99	$9.95
Granada & Sierra Nevada	£6.99	$9.95
Málaga	£5.99	$8.95
Orkney & Shetland Islands	£5.99	$8.95
Skye & Outer Hebrides	£6.99	$9.95

North America	UK RRP	US RRP
Vancouver & Rockies	£8.99	$12.95

Australasia	UK RRP	US RRP
Brisbane & Queensland	£8.99	$12.95
Perth	£7.99	$11.95

For the latest books, e-books and smart phone app releases, and a wealth of travel information, visit us at:
www.footprinttravelguides.com.

footprinttravelguides.com

Join us on facebook for the latest travel news, product releases, offers and amazing competitions: www.facebook.com/footprintbooks.com.